CHASING
THE
INSIGHTS

A Practical Guide to an Experimental
Approach in Digital Marketing

VINCE WARNOCK

ATG PUBLISHING

CHASING THE INSIGHTS

Copyright © 2019 by Vince Warnock.

For information contact :

ATG Publishing

ATG@chasingtheinsights.com

http://www.chasingtheinsights.com

ISBN: 9781075680533

First Edition: July 2019

10 9 8 7 6 5 4 3 2 1

"All life is an experiment. The more experiments you make the better."

Ralph Waldo Emerson

CONTENTS

Chasing the Insights

ACKNOWLEDGEMENTS

Writing a book is a lot harder than it sounds. I love the way Ann Handley put it in *Everybody Writes*. "Writing a book is a lot like birthing a Volkswagen." Now, I can't say I know what giving birth to a vehicle is like, but if Ann's comment is anything to go by, my guess is that it involves a lot of self-doubt, anxiety, and constant rewrites. That being said, I can honestly say that writing this book has also been one of the most rewarding and cathartic projects I have ever embarked on.

As I have gone through the journey of writing this, I am vividly aware that none of it would have been even slightly possible without the constant support of the strongest person I know, my beautiful wife Leanne. Babe, thanks for putting up with me constantly reading chapters out loud (over and over again with only minor tweaks). It's because of you I always want to better myself and I would not have been able to finish this book (or even be where I am today) without you. Love ya!

To both of our incredible children, Oriana and Jarvis. I am still in awe when I see how talented and compassionate you have both become. I know me and your mum are the parents, but I sometimes feel like the two of you have taught me so much. Seeing the world through your eyes makes me realise that anything is possible. Love you both!

A very special thanks to everyone who helped contribute to the book; you are all so ridiculously talented and it is an honor to have your wisdom and contributions in a book that has my name on it. Keep being awesome!

To my Cigna family, especially the senior leadership who constantly show me support and encouragement. The fact that you allow me to take chances with these crazy experiments has gotten me where I am today. Also, to my peers and colleagues, and of course to my team, who constantly keep me humble with your wisdom and talents.

To those who have inspired me over the years, I thank you. To the teachers who put up with this cheeky little know-it-all and yet still believed in me. To Ann Handley, whose words have driven me to finish this book. Ann, you were right... "I've got this!" And to Steve Lucas, who embarrassingly came up with a better name for this book than I had (I won't embarrass myself any further by letting you know what the original name was).

And lastly, to my sisters, especially to my sister Tracey. I miss you every day, Sis. Not having you around has left a giant hole in my heart. Love ya to bits!

EXPERIMENT

[noun ik-sper-uh-muh nt; verb ek-sper-uh-ment]
from Latin experimentum, from experiri 'try'

noun - a test, trial, or tentative procedure; an act or operation for the purpose of discovering something unknown or of testing a principle or supposition.

verb (used without object) - to try or test, especially in order to discover or prove something

geek - Something that inevitably results in someone getting bitten by a form of irradiated arachnid or bombarded with gamma radiation and obtaining supernatural powers (fingers crossed, one day... one day!)

INTRODUCTION

Welcome to *Chasing the Insights,* a book designed for you, the digital marketer. One thing I am pretty sure all digital marketers can agree on is that we live in a crazy world right now. The pace of change is staggering. You need look no further than the ever-changing face of marketing technology, the changes and controversies surrounding social media, and the incredible quantum of data available to us as marketers for proof of that. The list goes on and on and on. It is no wonder I often find myself pondering how on earth I am going to be able to keep up with all of this change.

To add insult to injury, consumer behaviour is also changing at a rapid pace. The techniques of old do not necessarily mirror what works today. Consumers expect a lot more from us now. If I generalise for a second here, they expect that we already deeply understand them, yet are not really comfortable with the amount of data we need to keep on them for that to happen. They also want things to work frictionlessly and to have radical transparency from brands. It is a lot to consider when planning out a digital strategy. As I said earlier, it's a crazy world!

So, with all of that in mind, I have a confession: "I often have no idea what the hell I'm doing."

Okay, full disclosure, I am only being partially serious with that statement (you will get used to this). Let me explain. You see, I occasionally find myself in the strange situation where we have just had a hugely successful campaign, and someone walks up to me and says, "Well done, that was fantastic. How did you do it?" To which I cheekily reply, "If I told you, I would have to kill you." This, of course, is Latin for, "Oh crap, I have no idea why it succeeded. I need to quickly look into the analytics so I have something to say and don't sound like an utter moron."

The good news is, I found out I am not alone. In fact, the more digital marketers I talk to, the more I am finding we all have the same fear. That fear of someone asking, "How come Tuesdays perform better than Thursdays?" or "Why did only five people enter our Facebook competition, yet when we posted that the weather was nice, we had thousands of engagements?" The reality is, we often get surprised. Analytics can tell us a multitude of different stories. However, often those stories can contradict themselves.

One way to think of it is as a form of a digital recipe:

Understanding a campaign

    1 cup of deep diving into the numbers
    2 tsp of changes in human behaviour
    1 pinch of seasonality
    1 smidgen of external factors
    1 tbsp of assumptions
    ½ cup of best guesses

Whisk vigorously and bake for one hour until someone walks over to tell you that they had forgotten to mention that the new TVCs went live last night and may result in a lot of new traffic online… sigh.

It's hardly Digital Masterchef!

The thing people don't seem to understand is that digital marketing is one part science, one part art, and a whole lot of what appears to be 'Aeaeae Artes' – otherwise known as the magic arts.

This is something that has consistently frustrated me. In

all truth, I do a pretty good job of making a fool of myself already without adding contradictory data, left-field factors, and the unknown into the mix. Well, there had to be a better way!

So, what now?

Well, the good news is that all of this frustration led me to start thinking about other industries that have the same problems: a ton of contributing factors and data that can be interpreted a number of ways. Then it hit me: the scientific community! This is their bread and butter. They constantly work with multiple variables and have to make sense of the chaos. And, of course, they do all of this through experimentation.

Now don't get me wrong, experimentation in digital marketing has been around for a while now, and I am in no way trying to claim that I am the only person who has come to this conclusion or approach. I am more telling you this to help you to understand a little more about how my brain works and how I came to the conclusion that an experimental approach to digital marketing will not only help us to achieve results but also to deeply understand what change is causing what effect.

So now that I have an approach, the next step is to dissect it into a practical application. And that, my good friends, is where this book comes in. The goal of the book is to provide a practical guide to help you transform your digital marketing into a results machine and to give you the confidence to no longer want to run away and hide under a desk in the fetal position every time someone tries to ask you a question.

As well as the background understanding of how to have an experimental approach to digital marketing, *Chasing the Insights* will also have a whole section on the mindset required to successfully implement an experimentation framework (an experimental mindset). And as if that wasn't enough, you can get even more excited, as I have dedicated the last part of this book to add the most amount of practical value I could. The last part of this book is where I have gathered together a number of experiments you can look to try through your own digital marketing endeavours. These experiments are a collection of ones I have tried myself, as well as a selection from other leading digital marketers around the world.

Next, let's have a look at how you can approach this book...

HOW TO READ THIS BOOK

Okay, before we get started, I am going to make a quick assumption here. I am going to assume that the fact you have already read past the introduction means that you are either my wife (being polite to me), OR you have a vested interest in digital marketing. If you are the first, then hey honey, you look fantastic today. If you are the latter, then welcome.

It's also worth noting that this book is written from the perspective of someone who looks after digital marketing within an organisation. If that is not you, don't panic and certainly don't put the book down. The fact is, the same principles easily apply to startups, agencies, not-for-profits, and the self-employed.

So how do you read the book? Great question (if I do say so myself)! The first thing to note is what I have already alluded to. This book is made up of three sections:

Section 1 - The Experimental Framework. This section is designed to help you have a structured approach to experimentation in digital marketing.

Section 2 - The Experimental Mindset. This section is designed to help you to be mentally prepared to implement experimentation and to show you how to get the most out of it.

Section 3 - The Experiments. This is the section where I get the help of some of the most talented digital marketers in the world to give you some practical examples of experiments you can try.

There are a number of ways you can approach the book. You can read it 'cover to cover,' although I warn you, it's not as exciting as you may think, and the ending is hardly *Animal Farm* or *The Old Man and the Sea*. Besides, this is one of the few books where everyone lives in the end.

You could also read it like a coffee table book. You could pick it up when you have some spare time (I have heard that some people have this abstract concept known as downtime). You could also pick it up and digest little chapters each time you need inspiration.

No matter how you approach it, there is a very deliberate reason that the subheading of this book has the words 'Practical' and 'Guide' in it. These words form the basis of how I approached writing this book.

Practical
[prak-ti-kuh l]

Adjective - *of or concerned with the actual doing or use of something rather than with theory and ideas.*
Synonyms - *empirical, hands-on, pragmatic, real, actual, active, applied, experiential, non-theoretical*

This book is a lot like advice from your dad: it is a little random, slightly cheesy, but somehow you know there is some wisdom in there somewhere. The challenge is, just like advice from your dad, it is useless unless you start to put it into practice. I'll give you a great example. There is a book that I absolutely love. It is called *Made to Stick* by Chip and Dan Heath. In fact, pause for a moment; if you have not yet read this book, I highly recommend you do! The principle of the book is simple: to explain ways to make ideas stickier.

After reading this book, I was genuinely inspired. What a great way to approach video production, content creation, digital display, etc. Yet, the way I used the book was all wrong. I read the book, understood the theory, got inspired, and then tried to remind myself of it next time I needed to create something. I thought to myself that the moment I read the book, everything I wrote would be a work of art, a virtual masterpiece of stickiness.

Okay, I am going to pause at this moment and not just because I am chuckling away at the sentence "masterpiece of stickiness," but also to let that sink in. I was genuinely inspired and it made me think of content in a completely different way.

Now fast forward a few months, and I am re-reading a piece of content I had written. This is when I realised that, despite the inspiration the book had given me, I had not used this great theory in practice at all! The content I had written was about as un-sticky as content could get.

This was unacceptable, so I tried again. This time I read the book, dissected the elements it was explaining, and would pause after each element to use it in practice. When I had finished writing my own content using this method, I discovered something I wasn't used to: I was actually pleased with my writing. This was the catalyst I needed to change the way I used this type of book. I would now keep the book alongside me, using it as a reference guide to ensure I was sticking to the method. The more I used these methods from the book, the more the theory became a habit, and the more it became a habit, the less I needed to constantly reference it.

So, this is a really good way to approach this book: practically! In fact, I really want to hear about your practical examples. Your successes and your failures. What worked for you and what didn't. Most importantly, what did you learn from those successes and failures? Hit me up on social media and tell me your stories.

The next keyword to help you approach this book is 'Guide'

Guide
[gahyd]

Verb - *direct or influence the behaviour or development of.*
Synonyms - *direct, steer, control, manage, command, lead, conduct, run, oversee*

This book is meant as a guide. Let's have a look at what that means for a second. I have a very good reason to create this book as a guide, and that is because no two digital marketers are alike. Sure, we all work in the same general vocation, but in reality, we all have different objectives we need to achieve, different sales processes, business models, problems, and obstacles to overcome.

I can lay out a foolproof method for influencing consumer buying behaviour, but if you are a marketer for a

Business to Business company (otherwise known as a B2B business), that is going to be of little value to you. However, the principles behind the theory, well, that is a different story. If you understand why a consumer behaves in a specific way, then those principles can be carried across to the key stakeholders in a B2B sales process.

A great example of this was in my own company. Back when we started Common Ledger, we were building a technology solution for accounting firms (pretty dry, I know). One thing we knew for certain was that the accounting industry is built on a foundation of trust, so breaking into the technology space when you are a young startup is particularly difficult. I knew I had to address this, so I started with a theory that I knew worked to build trust in the Business to Consumer, or B2C, space. That theory was around humanising the brand, putting a face and personality to the business. My theory (or hypothesis) was that people would find it a lot easier to trust something they can feel an affinity towards. So, I looked to a method I had used previously, which was to build a blog. The rules of the blog were simple. It could not be about the product we were building or even the value we knew it would add to accounting firms. Instead, we went the opposite direction; we made the blog all about the team and our journey. We showcased the toys we would buy for the office on our business trips, the large Darth Vader figure that would greet every visitor to the office. We talked about why we do what we do, the approaches we take, and the values we hold as founders. The family nights, the team dinners, the founders' boxing matches, and me almost falling out of a dingy dressed as Santa for the kids' Christmas party. All of the small things that we take for granted, yet make the team an awesome bunch of people to work with.

The goal, of course, was for people to feel the affinity towards us and then be open to doing a paid trial of our product. The effect was far bigger than we had first thought. I vividly remember sitting in front of a senior accountant for one of the larger firms. He had heard about Common Ledger through a colleague that read our blogs. I remember the moment he said to us, "We are taking a huge risk on you guys, but I really want you to succeed, so our resources are yours." A truly humbling moment and real-world validation that our approach had worked.

What I am trying to say is that you should try not to treat this book as absolute. Instead, treat it as a way to think about how you approach your own digital marketing.

The other thing I am conscious of is the fact that each of you reading this book are at different stages of your digital marketing journey. Some of you will be working with (or for) organisations that have a very mature digital marketing setup, while others will be completely new to digital. This is the exciting part about writing a book like this... I get the opportunity to talk to (providing someone other than my wife actually reads the book) people with a variety of experience and skill levels. Some of you will be far more experienced than me, while others will be fresh out of school. Either way, I really hope this book will be either a refreshing refocus, or that you will be devouring every aspect to bring your organisation into this crazy, topsy-turvy world of digital.

Just remember, I don't have all the answers... not even close. The answers, however, are there to be unlocked. All it requires is a well-structured approach to finding those answers, and YOU to unlock them.

In fact, if you only took two things away from this book, they should be that you should chase the insights, not the wins, and that experimentation allows for a compound interest approach to marketing. This means that you will get progressively better results as you keep pressing in.

"We don't chase the wins; we chase the insights."

THE EXPERIMENTAL APPROACH

So, now that you know the book is a practical guide, how do you then set out on this road to experimentation? The good news is that getting started is simple and, surprisingly, does not require a lab coat or Bunsen burner.

To get started, we first need to look at what is experimental methodology. And to look at that, we need to start by looking at what exactly an experiment is.

Experiments are the main method of inquiry in science.

Experiments are made up of three key features:
1. Control over the variables,
2. Careful and deliberate measurement, and
3. Using the data from that measurement to establish a cause and effect.

Experiments require the following:
- An initial **hypothesis.**
- An independent variable which can be manipulated. This is known as the **cause.**
- And a dependent variable which is measured. This is known as the **effect.**
- And finally, **control** over any extraneous variables.

Another key element in running an experiment is the ability to remain objective. The theory is that we should remove all preconceived ideas and biases about the outcome of an experiment. This includes removing the very thing we have become reliant on (particularly as you gain more and more experience in digital marketing), and that is our gut instinct.

Let's pause for a moment to understand what exactly our gut instincts are.

Instincts have long been thought of as "unqualified" reactions or responses to situations. However, to call them unqualified is a grave injustice. Our instincts are actually the brain performing advanced analysis and calculations based on the information you have on hand. Often, that information includes past experiences, knowledge that has been passed down, our own worldviews, and conscious and unconscious biases.

Think of our brain as the ultimate Big Data platform.

It is estimated that the human brain can store anywhere from 1 terabyte to 2.5 petabytes of data, although most computational neuroscientists estimate it to be closer to a range of 10 terabytes to 100 terabytes. If my brain is anything to go by, I am sure that it actually started at 100 terabytes when I was young, and slowly deteriorated down to 10 terabytes as I got older (okay, to clarify, the downward trend quote is not scientific fact, just an observation of how little I seem to be able to retain people's names, yet I still have the ability to quote every line from the original *Star Wars* trilogy which I first saw when I was 7).

On top of storing this staggering amount of data, our brain is also a computer more powerful than anything we have on this planet. This organic supercomputer spends most of its time analysing and running calculations on top of all of this data. So, theoretically, any gut instinct should be far more accurate than the outcome of any experiment we run.

A great example of gut instinct at play is a lucrative industry and possibly something you should consider if you ever wanted to change your career path. This example is a very well-paying occupation with a shortage of qualified candidates and a high level of demand. The only downside to this profession is when you have to explain what you do for a living to your friends and family at dinner parties. Quoting, "Oh, I look at the anuses of chickens all day" may make for an awkward evening.

What I am referring to (if you hadn't already worked it out) is the dying art of Japanese Chicken Sexers. Essentially, there are a number of people who have the job of trying to determine the sex of day-old chicks and hatchlings. The reason you would want to know the sex of a chick is not to know what colour to paint their hutch (and yes, that reference is only in here for comical effect; I am well aware that different colours for different genders is an archaic and outdated stereotype), it is instead so that large commercial hatcheries can separate out the females (or pullets) from the rest. To run the hatchery efficiently, they only keep a small number of males.

Trust me when I tell you, it is best at this point to not ask what they do with the male chicks (or cockerels).

"So why are skilled workers in this industry so rare? And

what the hell does this have to do with gut instinct, Vince? You said you would stay on track!" Don't panic, there is a point to my madness. You see, Japanese Chicken Sexers are a great example of how the human brain processes multiple inputs and data points to come up with a conclusion without actually understanding why.

You see, Japanese Chicken Sexers use a number of different factors to determine the sex of a chick. For years, people would try to analyse how the sexers would get such accurate results. When asked, the sexers found it very difficult to articulate how they came up with their conclusion. The reason they found it so difficult was due to the fact that there were multiple factors they were taking into account. There is the colour of the chick, the length of their feathers, and even how the anus would respond when you gently squeeze the chick to try to get them to excrete feces.

So instead of working on some advanced A.I. or algorithm to determine the sex, the sexers would take on apprentices who would work alongside them testing the chicks and coming up with their own conclusion. Once an apprentice had been corrected enough times, their brain started to factor in the multiple connections and factors to determine an accurate analysis. What appeared to be an almost magical gut instinct to those observing the sexers was in fact a large amount of data being processed by their supercomputer brains.

If you want to know more about this and the art of training intuition, I strongly suggest you read the book *Incognito* by neuroscientist David Eagelman. In the book, David looks at this fascinating occupation, as well as what the human brain does in the depths of its subconscious. It is a great read. Of course, make sure you finish reading *Chasing the Insights* first.

So why should we remove gut instinct from the equation? Great question! Essentially, the super powerful big data engine that we call our brain has a rather annoying flaw. That flaw is not in the cooling mechanisms or the distinct lack of Microsoft's Clippy (#bringbackclippy). The flaw is in the data we are loading into the big data engine. As mentioned, our brain uses a variety of various inputs for the data it analyses. Let's have a look at some of these inputs:

Experiences and observations - experiences and observations are just memories, and if you know anything about the human brain, you will know that memories are inherently unreliable. Every time we access a memory in our brain, the synapses that access the memory rewire themselves, effectively changing the memory. It's a scary thought, and I don't want us to get too far off track here, so when you have finished this book, you may want to go and look up the unreliability of witnesses in criminal cases. A great read is the paper called "The Neuroscience of Memory:

Implications for the Courtroom" by Joyce W. Lacy and Craig E. L. Stark (no relation to Iron Man). Essentially, police have a tough time trusting the information that witnesses give them due to the unreliable nature of our memories.

Learned (or passed down) knowledge - ANY knowledge that is learned or passed down comes from other humans or, as I like to call it, "flawed sources."

Then we have our own worldviews and biases - history will tell you that these views and biases do not always end well.

The point I am trying to make here is that our instincts are not always right. I mentioned earlier that a key element in running an experiment is the ability to remain objective. We mentioned that we should remove all preconceived ideas about the outcome of an experiment. In reality, this is next to impossible as, despite all of the negative aspects and risks involved in our own thoughts and instincts, they are inherently part of us and really difficult to remove.

So why then bring this up? Basically, I wanted to highlight this as a form of sense check. The key when running an experiment is to keep as open a mind as possible. You will often find that outcomes do not always go as expected and we need to be ready to either prove or disprove a hypothesis, not fall into the trap of trying to manipulate the results to show a positive outcome. Remember, disproving is just as valuable as proving. Our egos and cognitive biases should never get in the way of a good insight. We will go more into depth on cognitive biases later in the book (trust me, it is fascinating). The good news is that we have a whole section of the book dedicated to helping you have the right mindset for an experimental approach.

With all of that in mind, I have a process I like to follow to form an experiment. This is by no means the only way to approach it; it is more the method I have found effective for myself. I call it the C.H.A.S.E.R. method. Originally it was the P.H.B.E.M.R. method (Problem, Hypothesis, Brief, Experiment, Measure, Roll-out), but there is no way anyone is going to remember that, so thanks to an extensive read of the Thesaurus and lots of scribbling on paper, CHASER it is.

So, let's have a look at:

THE

C.H.A.S.E.R.

METHOD

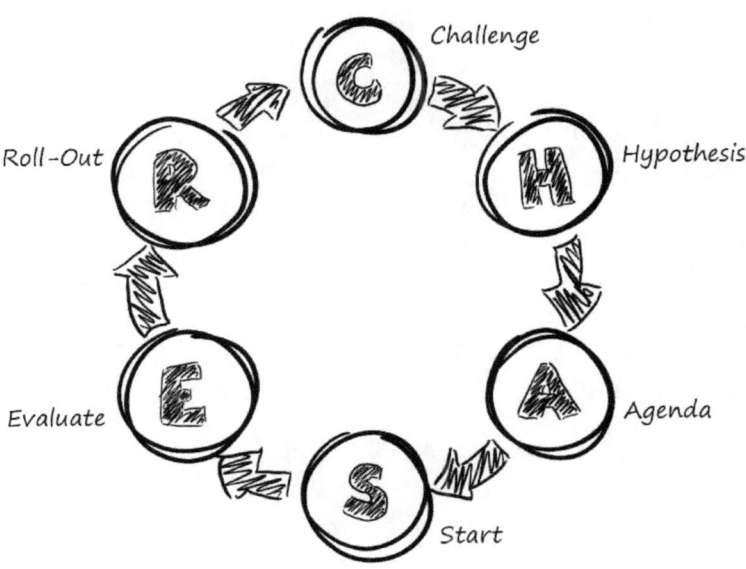

"The true method of knowledge is experiment."
William Blake

STEP 1:

CHALLENGE

CHALLENGE

Originally, I had called this section 'Problem,' as you will often find that problems are a convenient starting point for an experiment. However, the more I thought about it, the more I realised that this did not feel like it was the right description. That's when I paused and took a look back at some of the numerous experiments that I have run over the course of my career. I soon realised that there were a large number of experiments where the word 'problem' just did not fit. These are the experiments where something had been working well and we wanted to see if we could make it scale even further. Or experiments where we wanted to see if we could take an already well-performing process to see if we could make it more efficient. To call this a problem puts a negative spin on something that, in reality, was already performing well.

This is when it occurred to me that we were not actually looking at problems. Instead, we were looking at a combination of challenges, problems, and opportunities (maybe we should start to call them "Chaprops." Oayk, on second thought, after saying that out loud, maybe not). So this was the point when I came to the conclusion that the P should now be changed to a C and that we were no longer going to start by creating a problem statement, but instead should start by creating a challenge statement.

So why is this step so important? Can't you just start with a hypothesis and move from there? There are very simple reasons for this. Regardless of where you are in your digital marketing journey, if you were to sit down for more than five minutes, my hope is that you could come up with a dozen experiments that you may want to try. This then presents you with an interesting problem. Simply put, you cannot run all of these experiments at the same time! Remember, we are digital marketers, not mad scientists, after all. Instead, you need to focus on the experiment that will add the most impact or value first.

So how do you define this? That's easy, just look for the biggest challenge, problem, or opportunity.

I guess what I am trying to say is that the 'Challenge' step in the process starts you off with purpose. It requires you to have an understanding of how well (or unwell) your sales funnel and/or digital marketing efforts are performing. You need clarity on where the underperforming areas are and where you can focus to move the dial.

This also has the added bonus of making life a lot easier when managing up the line. When your CEO comes over and asks why you are focused on a particular experiment, you can cooly and calmly proclaim "sit back, relax, and let me tell you a story" while then explaining the background thinking behind the challenge, rather than the traditional method of nervously looking down at your shoes while muttering "we really thought it sounded like a good idea."

So how does this step work? How do we come up with these challenges, problems, and opportunities? Do we simply brainstorm a list of items? Well, kinda yes and kinda no. Essentially, this is the step that requires you to do the most amount of background work. This is where you need to have a really clear understanding of your online sales funnel, digital marketing campaigns, digital channels, social media metrics, analytics, SEO, SEM, SMM, CPC, BRB, LMFAO... Okay, apologies, the acronyms got away on me there and I over-acronym-ised (something that is a recurring issue within digital marketing, by the way. Maybe we will have to write a book on that one day).

Basically, all of that preamble was to say that you need to have a very clear picture of where things are at.

Now, at this stage of the book, it is very tempting to get sidetracked and do a deep dive into each of the areas you need the clarity on. However, I am determined to make sure this book has a singular focus on the experimental methodology (with the occasional and barely passable dad joke). So instead of talking to each of the digital marketing channels and the website sales funnel, I will give you some questions that you need to ask yourself. These are questions that should get you thinking about the right things (if you are not already), and will help you to identify the challenges, problems, and opportunities that will help you to start the C.H.A.S.E.R. method.

To do this, I am going to keep the questions at quite a high level and break them down into the key focus areas: Online Sales Funnel, Customer Journey, Retention, Digital Marketing Campaigns, Organic Search, Paid Search and Media, and Social Media. Remember, these are just a starter for ten. You really need to deep dive into each of the key areas of your digital footprint.

Have a read-through of the questions. Depending on the maturity of your digital marketing efforts, some of you will be able to easily answer all of the questions, while others will struggle at various steps (and for a portion of you, some steps will be redundant). As you read the questions, use them as a catalyst to start to think of areas that either need improvement or could do with some focus.

QUESTIONS

Online Sales Funnel:

- What is the primary purpose of our website?

- What defines a conversion?

- What is the path we want site visitors to go on to achieve that conversion?

- What does our sales funnel look like? Draw it on paper or on a whiteboard.

- What are the conversion rates from step to step in the sales funnel?

- What parts of our sales funnel are leaking?

- Do we have a lead magnet? How well is it performing?

- What are the negative friction points?

- What causes the most frustration for your users?

Customer Journey:

- What are the common buying triggers, events, or

conditions where customers search for a solution such as my offering?

- What are the common sales barriers and objections?
- What is the customer journey from awareness through retention?
- What is the purpose of that journey?
- How easy is our website to navigate?
- What reasons do your customers have to re-engage with you?
- What are the communication touchpoints through that journey?
- What is the purpose of each of those touchpoints?
- What channels do my customers prefer to be communicated in?
- How likely are customers likely to recommend my product/service to a friend?

Retention:
- How often are we engaging with our customers?
- For what purpose are we engaging?
- What's customer expectation on engagement?
- What is the customer sentiment on those engagements?
- What are our cancellation rates?

- Why are my customers cancelling?

- What is the cancellation process like?

- How often are customers defaulting?

- What is the process like when they default?

- How are the cancellations tracking over time?

- How do we capture customer feedback?

- When was the last time we spoke with customers to proactively get their feedback?

Digital Marketing Campaigns (including paid search and paid media):

- What are natural terms or questions that people would use to find similar content to mine?

- Who am I trying to reach (age, region, interests, etc.)?

- What part of the brain are consumers using when searching for my terms? Neo Cortex (conscious thought), Limbic System (emotional brain), Basal Ganglia (reptilian brain, e.g., instinctive responses)?

- What do my impression share and lost impressions look like?

- What is my ad relevance?

- How is my Click Through Rate compared to conversions?

- What is my landing page experience like?

- What are my competitors doing?

- Am I being smart with my retargeting efforts? What is the performance and experience like?

- How does my display performance vary across different devices?

- Am I making the most of the various targeting options available?

Organic Search:

- Which content on your site has the most unique visitors from organic search?

- What is the speed of my site on all devices?

- Which sites are backlinking to mine?

- Do I have any website errors?

- Do I have semantic markup on my website?

- Which sites have rich snippets for key questions in my industry?

- Am I blocking unnecessary pages from being crawled and indexed?

- Do my URLs contain relevant keywords?

Social Media Marketing:

- What is the purpose of our social channels?

- What social networks are we currently on?

- What are our engagement rates?

- What type of content performs best?

- What content frequency works best?

- What questions do consumers have that we can directly answer?

- What is my social persona?

- How quickly do we respond to messages?

- Am I A/B testing my social ads?

- What do our target markets use various social media platforms for?

- What are the main topics, categories, or messages that support your brand?

- What realistic resources do we have?

- What stage of the sales funnel does our social content target?

- How are social leads converting?

- What is the bounce rate on my site from social leads?

The goal here is for you to consider each of the questions and look for gaps in your knowledge. Take a brief moment to grab yourself a coffee or three (even a Tumeric Latte if you must) and contemplate each of these questions. As you work your way through them, the will hopefully start the thought process around where you have a challenge you want to address.

So, hopefully, you will now have some ideas around where you could start. If not, don't panic, you can easily just pick an area and start anyway. If you need help with which one to start with, I always maintain that it does not matter how much you push through a funnel. If the funnel is too narrow, then you get diddly squat out of it. So I would recommend you start with the online sales funnel.

The next part of understanding your sales funnel includes diving into your analytics. Once you have mapped out each of the steps in your funnel, you need to look at the conversion rates for your potential customers to transition from each step to the next. Once you have this data, you can then compare it to industry benchmarks to understand which steps are performing well or poorly.

This should now have given you a clear enough picture to be able to write a challenge statement. This is usually a simple sentence or paragraph that outlines the challenge, opportunity, or problem you wish to address.

Practical Working Example

As we move through the C.H.A.S.E.R. process, I am going to give you a real-world example to highlight each of the steps. The example I have chosen is a simple one and one that I have actually used in real life. It is a good way to showcase how the process can work well.

For this experiment, we looked at the conversion rates for visitors to one of our product pages through getting an online quote. This is an area that is quite high in the sales funnel and was performing adequately. Our challenge was to see if we could improve conversion rates. The theory was that if we increase the first step of the sales process, then more traffic would flow into the pointier end of the funnel which would, in turn, increase the numbers of conversions.

Our challenge statement would then read: "The conversion rate for traffic that lands on our product page through to completing an online quote needs to improve to drive more qualified traffic through to conversion."

Experiment: 2016-5-OSF

CTA Effort Quantification Experiment

Challenge statement: "The conversion rate for traffic that lands on our product page through to completing an online quote needs to improve to drive more qualified traffic through to conversion."

Let's move on to the next step.

STEP 2:

HYPOTHESIS

HYPOTHESIS

In the first stage of the C.H.A.S.E.R. method (The 'C' or Challenge step) we identified the challenge, problem, or opportunity that we want to address. In this section, we start to formulate the ideas, or hypothesis, that we think will address that challenge. These are the ideas that form the backbone of the experiment we are going to run.

First of all, though, why a hypothesis? Well, that part is easy. If we look at the scientific definition of an experiment, it tells us that the whole point of doing it is to test a hypothesis (or theory). Without one, we have no idea what we are trying to prove or disprove.

So how do we formulate a hypothesis? Well, I have some

good news for you here. This step does not have to be done alone. In fact, I would highly encourage treating the Hypothesis stage as a chance for collaboration. All it takes is for you to realise you don't have to have all of the answers, then swallow your pride and enlist the help of others.

Let's take a moment to look at the many ways you can formulate a hypothesis. At this point, it is worth noting that these are in no particular order, as everyone will have their own preferred method and you may find that different scenarios and challenges require different methods to find a good hypothesis to test.

YOUR OWN EXPERIENCE / IDEAS / GUT FEEL

This one is going to seem obvious and a little contradictory. Let me explain. In the beginning of this book, I started by telling you that you cannot trust your own gut instincts. At this point, I need to be clear that "not trusting your gut instincts" is in reference to analysing data and results. Your gut instinct can result in introducing bias to an experiment. With that being said, the area that gut instinct can prove invaluable is in the creation of a hypothesis. After all, you are the digital marketer, and this is your wheelhouse. Depending on your experience, you have a lot to bring to the table.

Often, a good hypothesis comes from the gut instinct you have when looking at a challenge. So sit yourself in front of a whiteboard or grab some blank paper and a pen, and start writing. Look at the challenge statement from the first step and throw your ideas down. Get those creative juices flowing and see what you can come up with.

THE WIDER INDUSTRY

The good thing about being a digital marketer is that you are not the only digital marketer. In fact, there are many others just like you around the world facing the exact same challenges that you are. There are always those that have paved the way forward and already tried many different ways to address various challenges. The key for us is to ensure that we keep pushing ourselves to find and test these examples. The best way to do this is to read, read, and read. I strongly suggest making it part of your daily routine to consume as many articles, books, podcasts, and YouTube videos as possible. I feel I should point out here that I am well aware that consuming podcasts and YouTube videos does not constitute reading, but I am pretty sure you got the point I am trying to make.

Something I firmly believe in is the Japanese concept called 'Kaizen,' which literally means "Good change" or

"Change for better." It is a simple concept that was first coined by Dr. W Edwards Deming (at least that is what the most common theory of its origin seems to be). Dr. Deming worked with the Japanese government after World War II to help rebuild Japan. So what is the concept? It is actually quite simple. It involves instituting a vigorous and consistent program of education and self-improvement. I know that this can sound a little too much like hard work, but, in reality, it just means keep reading and keep learning.

Personally, I have a scheduled time every morning (before even looking at emails… crazy talk, I know) to read articles that I have saved or bookmarked throughout the previous day. This is my time to try to learn new things or to open my mind up to creative thinking. I will even use the time to target a specific challenge or problem. Say, for example, I have an issue with open rates in emails. I will take a few days to read about engagement techniques for email marketing. I will read about the best practices and, most importantly, read as many case studies as I can.

The more information I consume from others, the better equipped I will be to challenge my own thinking. This is particularly evident when consuming other people's case studies. The beauty of case studies is in the fact that it is not some stranger's opinion or musings, it is simply fact-based evidence.

To sum up here, the net result of all of this information consumption is that you end up with a more creative approach to hypothesis creation.

SYNERGY SESSIONS

(now called PowerStorm Sessions)

Full disclosure, this by far my favourite method of forming a hypothesis (and not just because of the cheesy eighties name). So what exactly is a Synergy Session? Embarrassingly, it is basically just a fancy name for a brainstorming session. Okay, I need to elaborate here. Cast your mind back to a long time ago in a galaxy far far away… actually, in reality, it was not really that long ago, and the galaxy far far away was, in fact, our office. I remember having a conversation with one of my co-workers. We were both talking about a particular task that each of us had to do (but neither wanted to). We had been procrastinating and procrastinating getting started. The task had dragged on and on and, while talking about it, we came to the conclusion that neither of us had the mental energy alone to be able to tackle such a feat (and by 'such a feat,' I mean 'such a boring feat'). Both of us then had the idea to see if combining our powers made life any easier. It certainly did!

Having a structured time to work on a problem with

someone else meant that we could feed off of each other's energy. As one of us started to make headway with the problem, it would energise the other. An idea from one of us would spark the creativity of the other. We soon discovered that certain tasks were a lot easier when you work on it with someone else.

As much as we did not want to admit it, we realised that the principle of synergy was at play.

So, what is synergy?

Synergy
[noun sin-er-jee]
The interaction of elements that when combined produce a total effect that is greater than the sum of the individual elements or contributions.

So why were we so apprehensive to bring up the term? Simple, synergy is one of those terms that gets majorly overused in business circles. You know, like "blue sky thinking," "out of the box," "take this offline," and "tipping point." It's the kind of term that makes you want to reach across the table and slap your colleague hard across the face. The unfortunate thing about synergy, though, was that it was really the only accurate way to describe what had happened. So instead of fighting it, we scheduled regular sessions to tackle tasks like these and gave it the cheesiest name we could think of: "synergy sessions." We also set about to see if we could get as many people to subconsciously adopt the term as possible (that became a long work in progress).

I mentioned in the heading that we now call these sessions 'PowerStorm Sessions.' The reason for this is due to the fact that after years of running these Synergy Sessions (and trying really hard to get as many people to use the cringeworthy term), we came across one of the team at the digital agency Uprise. We were talking through running a Synergy Session and they mentioned that they too had tried to create a cheesy eighties-sounding name for their own version of a brainstorming session. They, however, had come up with the name PowerStorm Sessions. Pause on that for a moment. How could we possibly resist calling it such an awesome name? So from that day forth, it was written. "Thoust that storms their brains together shall from hence forth call them PowerStorm Sessions!"

So how does all of this business cheesiness help to create a hypothesis? Didn't you say you were going to keep on track, Vinny? Good questions. And trust me, we are still on track… there was a point to telling you all of this.

To use a PowerStorm Session to create a hypothesis is actually quite easy. You need to gather colleagues together. They can be a selection of your own team or, even better, a cross-functional team. Grab some frontline staff, call centre, the receptionist, IT team... anyone that can form an idea (which is actually ANYONE). Get them all together in a room with a big whiteboard and whiteboard pens that actually work, then talk them through the challenge statement and ask for ideas. Explain to them that there is no wrong answer and that even the most outrageous ideas can often stimulate creativity and help to hypothesise. As each idea is thrown at you, write it up and make a point of acknowledging the idea.

You will be surprised how quickly the energy stirs up and how quickly the silly ideas lead to actual gems.

As I mentioned earlier, I am a huge fan of this method. Not just because of the energy it creates and the ideas that come from it, but also because you cannot underestimate how powerful it can be to have multiple teams buying into the experimental process. Once you have decided on a hypothesis, do not be surprised if everyone that was in the synergy session keeps asking about the progress of the experiment.

A great example of how we do this on a regular basis is around our lead generation campaigns. We have learnt that having a PowerStorm Session with the front-line sales staff is invaluable. We talk them through the campaign we are wanting to run and ask them how the campaign idea could segue conversations with a consumer to a sales-based discussion. We ask them if the incentives would work with the target audiences and what information would we need to capture on a lead generation form to make converting a prospect a lot easier. When each of the teams has bought into a campaign, you will be surprised how well it performs.

CROSS-FUNCTIONAL CHALLENGE

Think of this as crowdsourcing your hypothesis creation. In this method, you are simply putting a challenge out to a larger group of people to see what ideas they come back with.

Obviously, the easiest way to do this is within your own company. It works on a similar principle to the PowerStorm Session, minus the concept of synergy. Essentially, you want to go out to the wider company with a challenge. Have some fun, put a prize on the line, and ask for people's ideas. As with the synergy sessions, you need to ensure you are clear about the challenge you want the ideas for. You also need to set aside time to sort through all the answers and comical responses as you try to pick a winner. To avoid the potential backlash you will get from some dominant personality types when they do not win, I would strongly suggest you put together a mini panel to select the answer that would best form your hypothesis.

It is also really important to communicate clearly throughout the process. Give updates and even highlight some of the more comical responses. When you announce the winner (and I know this is going to sound really obvious), make a point of highlighting some of the other ideas and celebrate the creativity of the office. I cannot stress this enough, as communicating clearly throughout the process will minimise any negativity and, more importantly, create a sense of ownership from the collective group. Similar to the Powerstorm Session, they will feel like they are part of the experiment and will buy into the results.

Another thing to consider with the cross-functional challenge is to expand it beyond your own company. One of the things I have tried in the past is to run a competition within closed Facebook groups. In my case, these are groups for local startups or tech and digital marketers. If you are not already part of these types of groups, I would encourage you to join. People are more often than not willing to help (in some cases, just so they can show off). Put a $50 Amazon voucher on the line for the best idea. Ask them to submit ideas and, if they have them, examples of where they may have seen it work. Again, be clear and transparent with the process, respond to every idea, and culture a positive atmosphere with the challenge.

You may want to be even bolder and open it up to an even wider community. Post a competition of your Facebook page on Twitter or LinkedIn. Be as upfront and honest as you can. Put a prize on the line and watch the ideas flow in. There are downsides to this approach to consider. You will receive a lot more entries, which means more administration. You will also undoubtedly receive negative backlash from some of the community. Trust me, people find the most random things to have a moan about: "You are asking for us to help solve a problem for only $50 when your executives earn x" or "We can't trust corporations who are only out to make a buck." In fact, you should see some of the weird complaints we have seen over the years. My favourite has to be a gentleman you wrote us a letter using coloured pencils to complain that in one of our TV commercials, we had a couple walking their dog in the park. It did not matter that the park was a dog-friendly one (I know because we had to ensure it for the permits), the gentleman had an issue that dogs in any public area could result in death. Essentially, he was worried that a dog pooping would leave residual fecal matter (even after being cleaned up) and if a person was to roll around in that specific area where the dog had pooped AND that person happened to have an open wound, the fecal matter could cause an infection that could result in death… wow! So make sure you have a clear comms strategy around this and realize that it is vital that you ensure you are prepared by running through every objection you can think of before posting the challenge.

COFFEE LINE TESTS

This method is an interesting one. It stems from when I was building Common Ledger. In the early stages of the company, we had little money and a need to get qualitative feedback from potential customers. We wanted a quick way to get feedback that did not break the bank, so I created Coffee Line Tests. Now to be clear, I am pretty sure I am not the first person to ever think of this, but at the time I had never heard of it and it seemed like such an epiphany. So, like any good marketer, I put some structure around it and gave it a name.

Coffee Line Tests can serve two purposes: one, to help spark ideas to form a hypothesis, and the other as a quick method of qualitative feedback to sense check any of your ideas you are looking to test. This is a great way to get face-to-face feedback (and all for the price of a coffee), but it does require more background work and a lot more extroversion than the rest.

So how does it work? Simple! Just rock up to a line in a particularly busy cafe and select candidates in the line that either appear to fit your target demographic or look like they are not in too much of a rush. Politely ask them if you could pay for their coffee in exchange for one to two minutes of their time to run some ideas past them. At this point, it is also a good idea to explain up front that you are not trying to sell them anything.

You will be surprised how many people are open to this. We have done this method a number of times and never failed to get good (and willing) participants. We often underestimate how much people like to feel like they are contributing. Plus, you know, free coffee.

The key to doing this successfully is in the preparation. To help you with this, I am going to separate the two types of Coffee Line Tests:

Hypothesis Creation - this is possibly the hardest of the two. Why, you ask? Well, because you do not want to go straight up to a consumer and ask them what you should do to solve a challenge. They have had no time to prepare, no time to formulate their thoughts, and at this stage are not even familiar with your industry or the challenge you are wanting to address. Instead, you want to get them to do what people do best… tell stories. Now to clarify, when I say stories, you do not want a "once upon a time…" or "it was the best of times, it was the worst of times…" No, I mean you want to get them to talk through something they have done and what they thought and felt as they did it.

Let me put that in context for you (trust me, this is a hard one to try to describe). Say, for example, you have a solus email that goes out to a portion of your newsletter subscribers. It has an offer that would be too good to miss out on... yet... only 22% of your subscribers open the email. In some industries, that is not a bad open rate, but your thinking is that this offer is good enough to warrant a significant lift in open rates. So that is your opportunity or challenge. To help formulate a hypothesis to test, you decide to use a Coffee Line Test.

Because you are trying to formulate a hypothesis, you do not want to just put a printout of an email inbox in front of them and ask which one they would open. No, instead you want to ask them to talk through a recent solicitation email they received. Get them to talk through what attracted them to the email... was it because it was from a trusted supplier? Was it because they had made a recent purchase there? To the best of their memory, what did the subject line say (note, it is not important that you get the exact wording; it is more important to get their interpretation, as that is the part of the subject line that stuck)? Did they use emojis in the subject line? What happened when they opened the email... what did they expect/feel?

Take note of the story. Record it on your phone if they are comfortable with you doing so. In their story is a wealth of insights. The various points that they remember are the gems that are going to help you form a hypothesis.

Now obviously, the example I used is a relatively simple one for people to remember (well, hopefully). For more complex scenarios, I would encourage the use of a type of sort card analysis (not traditional sort card analysis; instead, you want a simplified one that is more designed to help structure their thoughts). An example of one we use quite often is 'information source' cards. For this test we have a number of cards that list out each of the sources you may use to find to research a purchase you are going to make such as: Internet, print media, friends, family, TV, radio, etc. The goal is to get them to place these in order of how they would use them to research a topic. The order of the cards is less important than the story they tell while talking you through why they are in a particular order.

Another example of sort card analysis for this context is 'statement' cards. You have a number of cards with statements about what could be important when purchasing a product or service related to your industry. These could be statements such as "discounts on my purchase," "the product has an extended warranty," "I get a choice of optional extras," etc. With this one, you will get them to prioritise this into 'important,' 'nice to have,' and 'not important.' As with the previous example, the order is less important than the narrative as they explain why each of the statements is placed into the relevant prioritization.

Hopefully you now get the gist of how you can use this method to open up dialog with the participant. Remember, your best friends will be the following statements (use them as much as possible): "Talk me through why you have placed x there," "Tell me more about that," "Why is that?" and sentences to that effect.

Hypothesis Feedback - this type of Coffee Line Test is a little different and technically does not help with creating a hypothesis. Wait... what?! Why would you include it then, Vinny? I thought you were going to try and stay on track? Relax, relax, trust me, there is a point to this. Using a Coffee Line Test is a great way to get qualitative feedback to sense check your hypothesis.

Let me explain.

Say, for example, you have used one of the other methods of hypothesis creation. Let's use PowerStorm Sessions as an example. You have run a PowerStorm Session with a number of frontline staff and come up with around twenty ideas that you could use as a hypothesis to test. Maybe three of those are really solid ideas and a couple more are crazy enough that they might actually work. This leaves you with a problem: which one do you start with? You could just stagger them and eventually run all five of these ideas, but in reality, you only want to run one at this stage then move on to another different type of challenge. Instead of having to play an aggressive game of eeny meanie miny mo, you could simply do a graphical representation of each of the ideas and test them with consumers in a coffee line. The trick here is to not ask them what they like or which they prefer. Instead, what you want to do is to get them to tell you a story, maybe get them to describe the graphical representation to you. Get them to talk through what they are thinking and feeling. In reality, this may still give you two or three different options, but you can easily start to see which option may have an edge over the others purely from how they talk about each one.

Let me give you another example of this type of Coffee Line Test. Say, for example, you want to run a lead generation campaign on Facebook. You have run your PowerStorm Session and, from it, you have five different ideas for both a theme and an incentive. When you cast your eyes over the five ideas, you can see the merit in each of them. Now comes the tricky part: how do you know which one to try first? Jump in a coffee line with a rough sketch or mockup of each of the themes with their corresponding incentives. When you are running through the ideas with the consumer, ask them to describe each campaign. As they describe it, take particular note of the language they use, the excitement (or lack of) in their voice. Ask them what they feel when they see the campaign. You will be surprised at some of the feedback. I have had campaign ideas that on paper sound amazing but, when tested with consumers, turns out there is little motivation for them to engage with the campaign, or they did not realise that the campaign was actually asking them to do anything; they thought it was just an ad and were unaware that there was an action required for them to enter the competition.

This is a very easy and cost-effective way to sense check your assumptions before deciding on which hypothesis you want to test.

See what I mean? There was a very good reason to go off on a tangent. If you have a little faith, I will keep us all on track, despite the temptation to start talking about obscure *Star Wars* theories and which superhero deserves their own movie (did I hear someone say Moonknight?... Black Widow?... no?... okay, back to the book then).

So, there you have it. In this chapter we have worked through a number of different ways to help you create a hypothesis test. At this point in the book, I am keen to hear which ones you feel would work for you, but as this is a book you are reading, and books don't have ears, I can't actually hear your feedback. This is probably a good time to take a deep breath and hit me up on social media to let me know your thoughts. I am keen to hear if any of these methods work for you, or if you tried them and they absolutely failed (feel free to yell at me). At the very least, it will let me know that at least one person has read the book this far.

Practical Working Example

As we mentioned at the 'C' step in the C.H.A.S.E.R. process, we are working through a real-world example to highlight each of the steps. Let's continue by adding the 'H' step:

After running a PowerStorm Session, a number of ideas were floated to test as a hypothesis to increase conversion rates from your product page visitors through to completing an online quote.

Some of the top ideas that came from the synergy session:

- Create a sense of urgency by putting a timer on the call to action (5 minutes remaining to get an online quote).

- Quantifying the effort required to complete an online quote by changing the wording of the call to action from "get an online quote" to "get an instant online quote."

- Using fear by changing the call to action to read "if you do not get an online quote now, we will kill a puppy."

- Switching the call to action to a timer-based pop-up

modal that fills the screen after 15 seconds and asks them if they are ready to complete an online quote.

- Add a social proof element to the call to action. Next to the "get an online quote" button, add a section that states how many people have completed an online quote that day.

After testing these ideas in a Coffee Line Test, two of them made an impact: quantifying the effort required and adding social proof.

You have decided that the effort required to add the additional social proof element would delay the hypothesis test, so you've decided that the first experiment you want to try is the quantification of effort.

Your hypothesis is now: Quantifying the effort required to complete an online quote will result in a higher conversion rate. To test this, we are going to change the wording of the call to action from "get an online quote" to "get an instant online quote."

Experiment: 2016-5-OSF

CTA Effort Quantification Experiment

Challenge statement: "The conversion rate for traffic that lands on our product page through to completing an online quote needs to improve to drive more qualified traffic through to conversion."

Hypothesis: Quantifying the effort required to complete an online quote will result in a higher conversion rate. To test this, we are going to change the wording of the call to action from "get an online quote" to "get an instant online quote."

STEP 3:

AGENDA

AGENDA

Agenda is my 'Thesaurus-friendly' term for writing a brief. This is also the stage where a lot of people tend to skip this step and perform an experiment without it. This is partly due to the perception that it is not important or a waste of time. I would argue, however, that this step is critically important for a number of reasons.

CLARITY

Having a written brief helps to give you clarity and remove doubt. Trust me, you will be surprised how many times you find yourself coming back to your agenda to remind yourself why you are doing what you are doing, especially when the experiment is not panning out the way you had initially thought. Having a written brief not only helps you focus on what you are trying to achieve but also helps to keep you in an experimental mindset (and, let's be honest, stops you from freaking out about failure). We have a whole section on the experimental mindset coming up. You will soon start to see what I mean as we deep dive into the mentality required to run constant experiments.

WIDER VISIBILITY

I cannot stress enough how important having a written agenda is, as it gives your team visibility on what is actively happening at any point in time. Where this really shows its worth is when you have multiple parts of the business trying to make improvements to your sales performance. A good example is when you have an IT team making changes to optimise an online form. They want to see if they can reduce drop-offs at a certain point of the form by restructuring the layout of the page. At the same time the IT team are working on this, the marketing team are changing some copy on the product page to try and solve the same issue by providing more context on the page. If there is no visibility on what changes are being tested at what time, there is a potential that you will see either false positives, false negatives, or each department's changes cancelling each other's out and seeing no change at all. Trust me when I tell you this, and this is embarrassing to admit, but it has happened to me more than once before. I can honestly say that there is nothing more confusing than trying to understand the results of a test that contradicts itself (plus, it's damn embarrassing). So writing down the agenda for the team and wider business units to see is critical in trying to control any extraneous variables.

MANAGING UPWARDS

A written agenda is also going to be a valuable tool to help manage up the line. Let's face it, not all of us have the luxury that I currently have. I work for a CEO and board that are not only open to change and the risk that change presents, but they actively encourage it. So how does having an agenda written down help you to manage upwards? You will be surprised. Just having a clearly visible record of what is being tested in market will give them a comfort level to know that there is momentum (do not underestimate how important this is).

Another thing you may want to consider to complement the agenda (and help with upwards management) is a workflow visualisation tool such as a Kanban board to give a quick visual representation of what is in market at any specific time. I won't go into too much detail on how a Kanban board works here (as I feel it would take us down a rabbit hole), but you can easily Google "workflow visualisation methods" or "how to structure a Kanban board" without my help. Basically, a combination of a written agenda and a clear visual way to see what is in market at any specific time will help your senior management team have visibility on the momentum that is happening.

Additionally, it gives them something to talk about with you. In fact, the downside is that you will likely see a sharp rise in the amount of time they spend in your area. They will often ask how it is performing? What is your gut feel on what the outcome may be? Have we considered X instead of Y? What are your key learnings so far? They become part of the process, which is really important. As you can probably imagine, this is both a blessing and a curse (unless you are my boss, then I swear, it is only a blessing... phew, I think I got away with that one).

ONGOING RECORD

Keeping written agendas for all of your experiments will give you a record of what worked, what didn't, and provide an ongoing journal of knowledge. Where this really shows its worth is when you have new people joining your team. The agendas provide a lot of background info on why pages, forms, campaigns, and media are set up the way that they are. This means that a new team member can clearly understand the thinking behind various decisions and will mean they are building on an established and proven foundation. It also provides a valuable resource should the unthinkable happen… you get hit by a bus or leave to pursue a career in macrame making (don't laugh, it could happen).

Now that you know why you should write an agenda, how do you go about writing it? Great question! Basically, you want to take the problem statement from the C stage of C.H.A.S.E.R. and the hypothesis from the H stage and write them into a mini brief.

The key is to not go overboard here. You do not want to write an in-depth paper or pages of explanation, just a simple one-page document that outlines the following:

- *Challenge statement* - we have covered this in the previous sections

- *Hypothesis* - again, this was already covered in the previous sections

- *Approach* - a brief explanation of how you are going to conduct the experiment

- *Duration* – length of project and start date

- *Key variables* - write down the cause, the effect, and the control. In other words, what you are testing and what remains constant

You then want a blank area of your page where you can record the following key elements as you work through an experiment:

- **Benchmark metrics** - make sure you record the metrics before you start the experiment

- **What does success/failure look like?**

- **Results** - an area to write down the results of the experiment

- **Insights** - record observations, surprise outcomes, or anything you have learnt through the experiment

- **Outcome** - what the final outcome of the experiment is

I have seen many different variations on the written agenda, and the key is to make sure that you have the right information and that it works for you.

Practical Working Example

Let's continue with the real-world example by writing up what the agenda will look like:

Experiment: 2016-5-OSF

CTA Effort Quantification Experiment

Challenge statement: "The conversion rate for traffic that lands on our product page through to completing an online quote needs to improve to drive more qualified traffic through to conversion."

Hypothesis: Quantifying the effort required to complete an online quote will result in a higher conversion rate. To test this, we are going to change the wording of the call to action from "get an online quote" to "get an instant online quote."

Approach: Run an A/B test using our A/B testing tool. The 'A' version will have the current call to action button ("get an online quote") and the 'B' version will have the new call to action button ("get an instant online quote").

Duration: Four weeks starting on March 23rd. The exceptions will be if we can gain statistical significance earlier than the four weeks, where we can shorten the experiment. Or if we do not have statistical significance at the end of the four weeks, then we will review and make a decision on whether to extend the experiment.

Key variables:

- *Cause* - Call to action button change
- *Effect* - The percentage that converts (conversion rate) to completing an online quote
- *Constant* - Number of unique visitors to both the A and B versions of the product page
- Channels that the unique visitors came from - to ensure we are not skewing the data with higher- or lower-quality leads in either the A or B versions
- Channels that the conversions came from - to compare

with the product page channels

Benchmark metrics:

- Weekly unique visitors to the product page of xx,xxx for the previous month (sorry, cannot give out that info in this book, as this was a real-life experiment)

- Weekly unique visitors to the product page of xx,xxx from the same period in the previous year (again, apologies, but cannot let you see that far under the hood)

- A conversion rate of 35.43% (pretty sure I won't get in trouble for this one)

What does success/failure look like?: Either an increase in the conversion rate (proven hypothesis) or a decrease in the conversion rate (disproved hypothesis)

Results: To be added at the conclusion of the experiment

Insights: To be added at the conclusion of the experiment

Outcome: To be added at the conclusion of the experiment

Step 4:

START

START

I debated for a long time whether to include this as part of the process. The reason I debated this for so long was that the act of actually starting the experiment sounds so damn obvious. It is undeniably hard to disagree with this statement; however, I want to include it for a very simple reason (and not just because the C.H.A.S.E.R. approach would be C.H.A.E.R. without it).

The reason we need to include it is that you need to actively 'Start' an experiment. Not only start, but you also need to commit to seeing the experiment through. Part of the Agenda stage of the C.H.A.S.E.R. approach was to set a timeframe that the experiment will be in market and to set a start date. Once you have that start date, you really need to commit to it.

We will cover this more in the experimental mindset chapter of this book, but you will often find that external factors will try and take priority over running the experiments. Either that, or a sense of urgency will try to force you to abandon an experiment and instead try using a sledgehammer approach to quickly move the dial on a specific metric.

Having 'Start' as a definitive step in the process reminds you that it is all well and good identifying a challenge, formulating a brief, and putting it all down on paper as an agenda, but if you don't actually start the experiment, you will gain nothing.

It also reminds you to stick to the duration you set in the agenda stage. In fact, this is probably a good time to define the rule sets around duration. The goal of any experiment is to run it until you have a definitive answer. What I have found over the years is that the duration is never clear-cut and, often, experiments will need to be extended or cut short.

The best way to set a duration is to initially do a best guess of how long you think it will need to run based on the number of data points you will capture in that timeframe. Let me give you an example. Say you want to run two different experiments. One of the experiments is to try a different type of incentive for a Facebook competition. You are expecting at least 2,000 entries. Obviously, you would get a lot more data from this experiment than one where you want to double the number of people that download a specific PDF from your site from 5 to 10. You will need to run the PDF experiment a lot longer than the Facebook competition. So the key is to choose a starting point for the duration and allow yourself exceptions.

Generally, I fit most duration exceptions into the following categories:

Duration complete, statistically significant (DCSS)

This one is obvious; you find that you have reached the end of the set duration and there is enough data or learnings to draw a conclusion. This conclusion could be either that the hypothesis was proven or disproven.

Duration not yet complete, statistically significant negative response (DNSS-)

This one is a little trickier. This is where the experiment has not yet completed its duration, yet you have seen a definitive outcome in the negative sense. In other words, the outcome was that the experiment showed disastrous results early on in the experiment. I would try to tweak the experiment at least once to see if you can learn anything on the fly. If the experiment is still showing a strongly negative response, then consider abandoning the experiment.

Duration not yet complete, statistically significant positive response (DNSS+)

This is where the experiment has not yet completed its duration, yet you have seen a definitive outcome in the positive sense. In other words, the outcome was that the experiment showed strong results early on in the experiment. In this case, I would suggest you hold on for the full duration of the experiment to see what you can learn from the positive result. The temptation here is just to roll the experiment out as a Business as Usual (BAU) approach.

Duration complete, not yet statistically significant (DCSN)

This scenario is where we have run the full duration for the experiment but, as of yet, do not have enough data or learnings to draw a definitive conclusion. This one requires you to do some back-of-the-napkin calculations as to how long it will be before you see statistical significance, then weigh it up against your other priorities. If you feel that you could get a good dataset from extending for a short period of time, then do so. Otherwise, you will need to review the experiment and consider pulling the plug before you can get enough data.

So, there you have it. We have covered the fact that you need to make a definitive start to the experiment and have a clear view on the duration. Another thing that we mentioned earlier is that you need to constantly remind yourself that the benefit of the experimental approach is not so much in the result, as in the insights or learnings. This is why this step is so important: make the experiment 'not negotiable.' Set that target date and duration and commit to it.

Practical Working Example

In our practical working example, we have already identified the challenge that we wanted to address, created a hypothesis to test that will address the challenge, and we have written an agenda outlining how the experiment will work. With our practical working example, we have kind of cheated and added our start date and duration into the agenda already. So at this stage, I am going to summarise the experiment with the following:

Experiment: 2016-5-OSF

CTA Effort Quantification Experiment

Challenge statement: "The conversion rate for traffic that lands on our product page through to completing an online quote needs to improve to drive more qualified traffic through to conversion."

Hypothesis: Quantifying the effort required to complete an online quote will result in a higher conversion rate. To test this, we are going to change the wording of the call to action from "get an online quote" to "get an instant online quote."

Agenda: Complete

Start: The experiment will be run for four weeks starting on the 23rd of March. The exceptions will be if we can gain statistical significance earlier than the four weeks, where we can shorten the experiment. Or if we do not have statistical significance at the end of the four weeks, then we will review and make a decision on whether to extend the experiment.

STEP 5:

EVALUATE

EVALUATE

The next phase of the process is the evaluation and is quite possibly the stage of the process that you have to pay the most attention to. The reason for the increased attention in this stage is because this is where the gold is. Think of the data points and feedback you gather throughout the experiment as the raw minerals that you can chip away at to find the gold (or insights). I would just like to point out, that in that analogy, that would make you Jebediah, the crazy old coot that lives down in the mines... food for thought.

So the big question (other than how Jebediah lost his mind and why did he move from his swanky apartment down into the mines?) is how do we run an effective evaluation? That's an interesting question.

The answer lies before the experiment has even begun. This is because you will need to work out what your benchmarks are before you can start any experiment. Now, I know this sounds really obvious, but setting the benchmarks is critical! This is the starting point to understanding if the experiment is having a positive or negative effect.

Let me explain it with an example: if you are doing an experiment to increase your paid reach on Facebook (without the obvious one of tucking lots of hundred-dollar bills into Facebook's G-string), you will first need to understand what your previous paid content was getting on average for the same spend over the same timeframe.

In this scenario, you will need to know the obvious metrics and benchmarks, including:

- Number of followers at the time
- Actual reach of the paid post
- Percentage of organic reach achieved on the post
- Timeframe the paid media was in market
- Amount spent to boost the content
- Engagement type breakdown (Likes, Shares, Comments, whatever you call those emoji things)

Then you have the less obvious ones:

- Type of media used (image vs video vs animation vs text, etc.)

- What was the nature of the post (theme, topic, sentiment, etc.)?

- Any external factors that may have skewed the benchmarked results (such as media attention, public holidays, heightened awareness of the topic)

You can see what I am trying to do here. Gathering all of this type of info will enable you to understand the exact environment of the 'Control.'

All of this will enable you to do two things: understand what the variables are (and to mitigate any effect they have), and have a clear picture of where your benchmarks are. Once you have all of this information, you can then look to measure against them.

The next thing you need to do in this step is to keep a scorecard of the results. The concept of a scorecard is pretty simple. You basically want to clearly see what your benchmarks are and where the running results of the experiment are. These results are all based on the metrics you are measuring against (as per the previous example).

There are obviously many (and I do mean many) ways

you can do this. In all honesty, I am not too concerned with how you design your scorecard; I am more wanting to ensure that you keep regular track of the results. The key to a good experiment is to have clear visibility of the progress and to know when the experiment is performing well or performing poorly. The one thing I can tell you is that Excel or Google Sheets will quickly become your best friend!

Now that the experiment has started, there are a few things to note. Firstly, do not be surprised if you get some wild results at the beginning of an experiment. I have no scientific understanding of why this is (which is likely because I have never really given it too much thought), but what we have found is that experiments tend to have quite varying results at first, then level out over the course of the experiment. This is particularly evident in smaller experiments. When you do not yet have enough data for it to be statistically significant, then you need to look at the regular results with a critical and patient eye. There is a term for this which will we will cover in the Open-minded-ness section of the book. It is called the Hawthorn Effect - more on that later.

So how do we trust the results we are seeing?

Well, as mentioned in the 'Start' part of the process, statistical significance is your friend. For an effective analysis, you will need to ensure you run the experiment long enough to gather enough data so that you are comfortable that the results are a good and fair representation of what is happening. With smaller sample sizes, one factor can skew the data to ridiculous results. You need patience and an experimental mindset to not give up at this stage (more on that in an upcoming chapter).

Once you have run the course of the experiment, you need to do two things (although I highly recommend adding a third to the mix):

Analyse and summarise the data:
This is where you need to finish filling in the scorecard and produce the final results. Once you have done this, you can easily compare them to the benchmarked results to see if you have had a positive or negative result.

Note down all of your insights and findings:
The data from the experiment is only one factor. The real gold is in them thar insights (trying to channel our good friend Jebediah the gold miner again). Take note of your observations and anything that surprised you about the results. Look for inconsistencies and anomalies as well, as often they can hide little nuggets of wisdom. This is a really important step, as having a recording of your thoughts and insights will be really valuable when you look back on various experiments you have run.

At this point, you should take a step back, pause, and reflect on everything you have recorded. Does it make sense? Are you confident enough with the findings? Have you recorded every thought and insight?

This is also where the third thing I suggest kicks in. I strongly suggest you get a quick peer review. Often, we see what we see due to living in the experiment. Having an outsider review the data and findings can be a useful way to give you confidence in the results or to stop you from making an embarrassing conclusion. The embarrassing conclusion is something I am well-versed in. The number of times I have processed my thoughts out loud, only to realise that there was something obvious I had missed... oh, the embarrassment... oh, the humanity.

Practical Working Example

In our practical working example, we have already identified the challenge that we wanted to address, created a hypothesis to test that it will address the challenge, written an agenda outlining how the experiment will work, and started the experiment. Now we get into recording the data for the experiment onto our scorecard. Note, as per the agenda we created, this is an actual experiment that we ran, but I am changing the data from the experiment because this is commercially sensitive.

Experiment: 2016-5-OSF

CTA Effort Quantification Experiment

Challenge statement: "The conversion rate for traffic that lands on our product page through to completing an online quote needs to improve to drive more qualified traffic through to conversion."

Hypothesis: Quantifying the effort required to complete an online quote will result in a higher conversion rate. To test this, we are going to change the wording of the call to action from "get an online quote" to "get an instant online quote."

Agenda: Complete

Start: The experiment will be run for four weeks starting on the 23rd of March. The exceptions will be if we can gain statistical significance earlier than the four weeks, where we can shorten the experiment. Or if we do not have statistical significance at the end of the four weeks, then we will review and make a decision on whether to extend the experiment.

Evaluate:

	Unique visits	Quotes	Conversion rate
18th Jan	2,359	287	12.17%
19th Jan	2,154	240	11.14%
20th Jan	1,978	212	10.72%
21st Jan	2,673	298	11.15%
22nd Jan			
23rd Jan			
24th Jan			
25th Jan			
26th Jan			
27th Jan			

STEP 6:

ROLL-OUT

ROLL-OUT

Similar to the 'Start' part of this process, I debated whether to include this step. Most test and learn cycles are only three to four steps (Design, Build, Test, Learn). I really wanted to include roll-out as a deliberate step for a reason, and that's because it's a mental pause in the process to regroup and to establish what the next steps should be.

There are two main parts to the roll-out step. The first part of the roll-out is to establish what happens next. Based on the results and insights of the experiment, you want to put it into one of four categories:

- Complete - add to BAU (Business As Usual)
- Complete - dismiss from BAU

- Complete - inconclusive
- Complete - scale

Complete - add to BAU: This one is obvious. If you have proven the hypothesis, the next step is to include the changes you made to conduct the experiment in your day-to-day process. For example, let's say you made a change to the layout of a product page by bringing the call to action to the top of the page. Your hypothesis would have been that this will increase the percentage of visitors that convert to the call to action. If the results of the experiment show a definite positive result, then you will want to keep this change and roll it out for all product pages on your site.

Complete - dismiss from BAU: Another obvious-sounding one. This is where you have disproved your hypothesis during the experiment and do not want the changes you made to be included as part of your BAU. Using the previous example, if moving the call to action had shown a definite negative result (the conversion rates went down), then you do not want to keep the changes and, in fact, want to roll the call to action back to the previous state. A handy tip at this point is to remind yourself of the insights you have gained through the experiment (trust me, it helps with the anguish of disproving a hypothesis test).

Complete - inconclusive: This one is a little tricky. Unfortunately, not all experiments have a clear or concise outcome. Looking at the previous example, this would be where the conversion rates stayed approximately the same as the benchmarked figures. What you do with this category depends on you. I would look at each experiment on its own merit. As an example, if you had made the changes to the location of the call to action and the results had shown no change, you could decide that you wish to roll it out as BAU because the pages flow better with the new CTA position, OR you could decide to reject the changes due to the fact that consistency is more important to your users. This is where experimental digital marketing differs from scientific experiments, as this is where I tell you to do the unthinkable: trust your gut.

Complete - scale: This is the most exciting category. This is designed for experiments where you have run a small experiment on a subset of your audience and the results have shown a definite improvement. This is the type of change you want to then apply to the wider audience to reap the benefits at a much larger scale. A good example of this is if you wish to run an experiment to test a new lead generation tool on Facebook. Your hypothesis may be that you will see a good number of quality (and low cost) leads coming through. If the experiment has shown a positive result, you could then determine that you want to put more money against the lead generation tool to generate more leads. Note: a key to this category is when you scale the findings, you want to ensure you keep an eye on the results going forward. Remember, not all positive experiments scale well.

The second part of the roll-out is to reset the benchmarks (you will be surprised how often people forget this step). At the beginning of an experiment, you had recorded a set of benchmark results. You want to make sure you have a record of what the revised benchmark figures are going forward. A good way to do this is to make notations in Google Analytics.

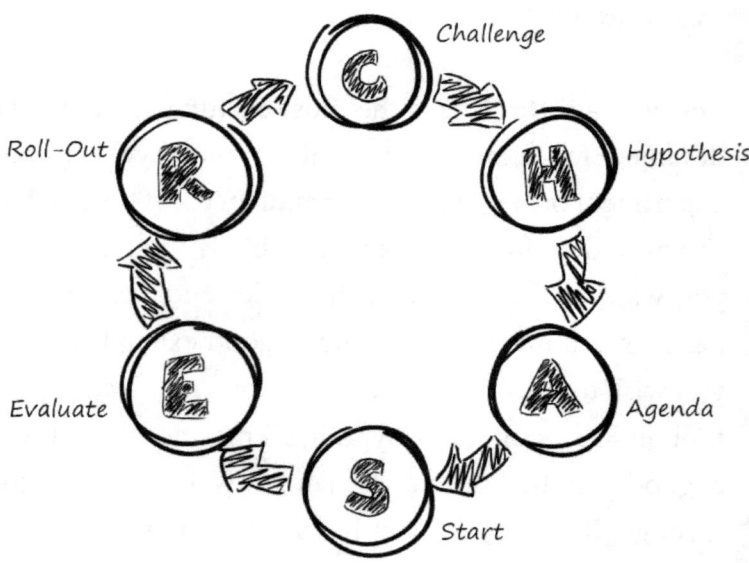

SECTION ONE SUMMARY

Well, that's it, my good friends. Not only have you made me feel good by reading this far through the book, but you now have (hopefully) a good understanding of the C.H.A.S.E.R. method for running an experiment. Before we get into the second section of the book, let's take a few moments to have a look at some of the key take-outs from the first section:

We don't chase the wins; we chase the insights - this is an important way to approach an experimental framework. In the next section of the book (aptly titled "The Experimental Mindset"), we will dive more into the mindset required for running experiments.

Do your homework - at the beginning of the C.H.A.S.E.R. method we highlighted the importance of knowing your digital channels and assets and the importance of understanding your digital marketing campaigns. The more you know and the more you deep dive into every aspect of your digital marketing, the more you will find it easier to identify the challenges you want to address through experimentation.

Control the constants - In the Agenda step of the C.H.A.S.E.R. method we talked about the importance of recording benchmark metrics. This is so that you have a full picture of every variable that can affect an experiment's outcome. By knowing the variables, it will enable you to better treat them as constants. Remember, the only variable we want at play is the cause and the effect variable.

Read, read, and read - A key element to the success of an experiment will be your ability to think differently and see beyond your tiny bubble of a world. The single best way to do this is to get other people's views and thinking. Of course, you get this from reading as much as possible. Make it a vital part of your daily routine.

Run a Coffee Line Test - Speaking of getting other people's views, what better way to do that than by talking directly with potential customers? Do not underestimate the power of actually talking to consumers. You will quickly find that they do not always think like you do. Plus, there is the added bonus of how positive you will feel after talking to Joe Public.

Run a PowerStorm Session - Thanks to the team at Uprise Digital, we have an awesome cheesy eighties name, now don't let it go to waste. Crowdsource your hypothesis creation by getting cross-functional people together to brainstorm. You won't regret it.

Now on with section two of the book...

THE
EXPERIMENTAL
MINDSET

"Life is trying things to see if they work."
Ray Bradbury

THE EXPERIMENTAL MINDSET

Before we get into this chapter, let's have a very quick recap. Previously in this book, we have covered why we would want a different approach to digital marketing. We looked at what an experimental approach looks like and what the C.H.A.S.E.R. method entails (Challenge, Hypothesis, Agenda, Start, Evaluate, and Roll-out). We even looked at some practical examples to see the approach and method in action.

This next chapter covers something that is probably more important than the methodology itself. Each of the things we have touched on previously has looked at very tangible and practical tools that you can have in your arsenal to help you have a different approach to digital marketing. If you stopped reading the book right here, you would certainly have a good practical guide to how to structure an experimental approach, although I would argue that you would not necessarily be guaranteed that this approach would be able to be implemented in your work environment. Besides, if you finished the book here, you would always be wondering how the book ended. Did the groundskeeper ever find true love? Did the kids discover what the glowing light at the pier was? And whatever happened to all the bees?

None of the previous chapters deal with the one constant that runs throughout all of your experiments, the one constant which will determine how well your experimental methodology is adopted by your team and the wider company. The one constant that could mean the difference between revitalising your digital marketing efforts or simply reverting back to what you are used to doing. You know, the same old same old. Can you guess what that constant is? Go on, take a punt! Yep, you are correct: YOU are that constant.

Okay, yes, that was a particularly cheesy and over-dramatic paragraph. But there is a reason for it. It is all true. YOU are the key ingredient to adopting an experimental approach, and if you have the right mindset, it can have a hugely positive effect.

Training yourself to have an experimental mindset will make you look at everything differently. You will start to question every process, campaign, every aspect of your digital assets and marketing. You will look for every opportunity to challenge your own status quo and to take risks. This is the ideal, the nirvana (I am really resisting the urge to say "Blue Sky" here) and, of course, the whole purpose for you reading this book. Digital marketing is a game of inches, not miles. Once you start to cultivate this experimental mindset you will start the momentum forward. You will be on your way to turning your digital marketing into a growth machine.

This game of inches can be thought of as the 'Compound Interest' approach to digital marketing. Each proven or disproven hypothesis and every insight you gain along the way will incrementally add to the overall success of your digital marketing efforts.

So how do we define exactly what an experimental mindset is? Well, this is where it gets tricky. I have been racking my brain looking for a good explanation to describe the type of mindset I am talking about, but it is easier said than done... well, actually, now that I read that aloud, I can see it should say "harder said than done," which is why I am struggling here.

The only way I could find to describe an experimental

mindset is to break it down into five key areas. These are the attributes that you can work on to adopt the right mindset. Note I said "work on." This is going to sound really obvious here, but changing the way you are wired is not an instantaneous process. One cannot simply decide to have an experimental mindset. It is something you will have to constantly and consistently work on (later in this section we talk about the Kaizen approach, and this approach to life will help you to keep this mentality). I can honestly say that I am still making a conscious effort to adopt these traits. I don't always get it right, but the more you work on them, the easier it gets. It is also worth noting that you will also find that aspects of these five attributes come easier to different people.

So, what are the four key attributes to an experimental mindset? They are (in no particular order) Fortitude, Curiosity, Confidence, and, lastly, Open-minded-ness (and yes, I made that word up).

Let's have a look at them...

ATTRIBUTE 1

FORTITUDE

FORTITUDE

[fawr-ti-tood, -tyood]
Noun - Mental and emotional strength in facing difficulty, adversity, danger, or temptation courageously
Synonyms - courageousness, valorousness, resolution, perseverance, spunk

Fortitude is an interesting one. It is the ability to push through, no matter what obstacles you face. It is that mental and emotional strength that, for some reason, certain people seem to naturally have. In reality, though, fortitude is just a mindset and, like any mindset, you can actively cultivate it. So how do we cultivate a fortitudinous mindset (you cannot physically see my face as I am writing this, but I have a huge smile right now, as I have been trying to find an excuse to use the word fortitudinous for some time)?

There are two key areas that help you to cultivate the fortitude you need to have an experimental mindset. These are Perspective and Cues, which I will explain shortly.

Perspective

Simply put, perspective is your ability to look at the larger picture, your ability to be able to step back from a difficulty or an adverse situation to enable you to have the strength to deal with it.

Let me give you an example. When my daughter was younger, she was an avid netballer. Every weekend we would be at the freezing cold courts with all of the other suckers... I mean parents, cheering the team on and standing ready with a slice of orange at halftime. One weekend, my daughter's team played a particularly aggressive team of mostly older girls. The game was going well and, despite how aggressive the opposing team were, they had not yet broken any rules. The game had just entered the last 10 minutes and the score was tight (the opposing team had a 1-point lead). My daughter was on defence and had just intercepted a pass when the player she had intercepted got a little upset. This is where the aggressive attitude of the opposing team took a turn. The girl decided that she was going to play the player instead of the ball. She stomped on the back of my daughter's foot, causing her to drop to the concrete. My daughter still had control of the ball and passed it off to another player before hitting the ground. When she got up, she had a huge gash on her knee and what seemed to me to be a considerable amount of blood running down her leg.

This is where I learnt an incredible lesson about the human spirit and what it means to have fortitude. My daughter did not even flinch. She was in obvious pain and you could tell that she was finding it difficult to put any weight on her leg (and I was finding it difficult not to run onto the court to look after her). Instead, she moved as fast as she could up court to apply more pressure to the opposing team.

Long story short (well, short-ish), her teammates got the points to secure the win and she kept pushing through until the final whistle blew. The second that whistle blew, she became very aware of how much pain she was in and the tears started to flow.

We had just witnessed what happens when someone has a different perspective. Instead of focusing on the pain or the blood running down her leg, instead of focusing on the injustice of the other playing stomping on her, she was focused on one thing and one thing only: the game. She was determined to play as a team and not let the side down. She was focused on finishing the game. All of this ensured that she could push through the pain and discomfort to keep playing. That day I honestly felt I had become the student and she was indeed the master.

Think about it, how many times have you seen little toddlers running along and fall over, only to just get back up and keep playing? The second someone asks if they are okay, they change their focus to what just happened and the tears start flowing. Perspective is **EVERYTHING!**

Have you ever noticed that some people seem to be affected by the smallest of things? Some people can fall short on a target and lose confidence and motivation to try again. "What's the point? I will only fail." Others can fall short then double down and knock it out of the park on the next try. It is all about perspective.

One thing you will find with an experimental approach to digital marketing is that we will often fail. Experiments will rarely go as we expect them, and if we lose perspective of why we are doing this, then we will lose our motivation and want to give up. We have to constantly remind ourselves that the goal of an experiment is to prove OR disprove a hypothesis. The whole point of an experiment is to chase the insights we will gain from it.

So how do we keep perspective? How do we remind

ourselves of what we are trying to achieve? There are a few tips that could help here. The first is obvious: we need to literally remind ourselves. It helps to make it visual. Write yourself a statement to put on the wall if it helps:

"The purpose of an experiment is to gain insights. This means proving OR disproving a hypothesis."

Feel free to modify the words to better suit you. For some people, it is enough to remind themselves as part of their morning routine; for others, it is something that they need visibility on during the day. It is really down to whatever works for you.

Another tip is to take helicopter time. And sadly, this does not mean that you need to schedule in regular time up in the air in an actual helicopter (although, how cool would that be!?!). What this means is that you should schedule some time each day or week (whichever you feel is necessary) to take a step back and look at how the experimental program is working and what you have achieved with it. This is something that I do not do enough, which is surprising, as every time I do, it totally re-energises me.

Taking the time to focus on the value you are gaining from the insights, taking the time to reflect on how far you have come, these are the things that will help to give you perspective. Who cares if one experiment is not going the way you thought it would? Especially when you have a dozen under your belt that have succeeded.

Perspective is an incredibly useful trait, not just when implementing an experimentation framework, but also for life in general!

Cues

What is a cue, you ask? Simply put, a cue is a form of signal. Think of it in acting terms. In the theatre, a cue is a signal to the actor or performer to enter the stage or begin a speech or performance.

So, what does this have to do with having fortitude, you ask (well, I am assuming you are asking. I mean, come on, it is a pretty abstract concept to tie to fortitude)? Think of it this way: Cues are not only used to signal that you need to enter the stage, but they can also be a signal to your brain that you need to trigger a routine for a habit. A good example of this is how putting on your activewear makes some people feel like they want to go for a walk; for others, it is how putting on pyjamas makes them feel tired. These are cues for your brain to enter into either exercise or sleep mode. How about when you have your first coffee in the morning or the sweet sweet smell of bacon? Both of these can be cues that you are mentally prepared to face the day. Damn, now I need to make myself a coffee and a bacon butty. Back soon...

...nom nom nom. Okay, it is quite difficult to give an overarching example of cues that everyone will understand. This is because all of us are wired completely differently. Each of us has our own learned cues that trigger certain mental states or routines.

Cues can trigger different mindsets and feelings. The trick is to learn to cultivate those cues. We need to learn cues that can create a mental state of readiness to be able to face any challenge.

Let me give you an example from history. Back in the 19th century, there was a Welsh-American explorer called Henry Morton Stanley. Henry was a complex man (that is my polite way of saying he was a bit of a dick, but his experience is useful in teaching a lesson on mental cues). Let's travel back to 1875 when Henry was tasked with mapping out the entire Congo River. This was no mean feat. Henry departed with 228 men on this intrepid journey and faced all manner of adversity and difficulty. They faced the constant risk of malaria and dysentery - both of which were fatal back in the old-timey days (as my son would put it). They faced starvation, drowning, and even natives shooting arrows at them. It took Henry and his men 999 days to complete the task and at the end, of the 228 men, only 114 men survived.

Henry was considered to be an incredibly self-disciplined man and would never have survived the journey if he did not have a lot of fortitude and inner strength. In fact, Henry had so much fortitude that the natives called him Bulamatri, or breaker of rocks.

So how did Henry have so much fortitude? Well, the explorer attributed most of it to a specific habit. Henry had a routine that he had himself (and his men) perform every morning. He would wake up and shave. That's it! It sounds so simple, I know, and is hardly a task that is required when mapping out the Congo. However, what Stanley had stumbled across was a way to get into the right mindset every day by using shaving as a mental cue. The act of shaving every morning caused Stanley to feel 'proper' (sorry, hipsters, his words not mine). Shaving also put Henry and his men in the right mindset to keep breaking through each day. It is incredible to think how well Henry used a simple routine to basically trick his mind into a specific way of thinking.

Now, it is worth noting here that, although this is a great example of using a mental cue to create a specific mindset, in no way should we go on to idolise this intrepid explorer. Henry was reported to be a horrible individual who was cruel to both his men and the Africans they encountered. It just made a great story to illustrate the power of the human mind and how we can use simple tasks and tricks to harness this power.

Cues are something that I use a lot in my own life. A good example of this is how I structure my office at home. Now, a warning is in order here because I am going to explain just how geeky I really am. I feel at the end of this you will either be scared, disturbed, or, hopefully, inspired.

So how have I set up my office? Great question. First of all, I have set up RGB LED lights behind my desk and monitors. If you have never heard of these before, they are basically strips of lights that you can change the colour of. I have them set up to work off of a remote control and have even connected them to my smart hub at home. This means I can set up a command on the smart hub so that when I walk into the office and say, "Computer, switch me to writing mode," the lights change to a green colour and the music turns on to a funky jazz playlist I have set up. Likewise, if I want to study instead of write, I can say "Computer, switch me to study mode." The lights then change to a blue colour and the music changes to a softer jazz. There are many other modes, including recording mode (for video work), creative mode, gaming mode, and more. The key thing here is that I use these modes to cue my brain to switch to a specific way of thinking. If the lights are green, I feel like writing... it's simple, and, for me, it works perfectly.

So, what does this have to do with fortitude? How can

setting up different coloured lights or music playlists help me to keep mentally strong when difficulties come?

Essentially, the plan is to train your brain to keep an experimental mindset. To keep focused on the purpose of the approach (the insights) and to train your brain to think differently. You need to train yourself to work off of cues. Unfortunately, I can't teach you what those cues are; you have to work that out for yourself. Start looking at times where you feel most resilient, where any difficulties simply flow like water off a duck's back. In these times, start to think about your environment, start to actively take note of the time of day, where you are, what you are listening to. Are you wearing activewear, casual clothes, or business attire? Your brain has already made a loose connection with these factors, and now you need to look at these factors to see which ones you use to replicate the feeling of fortitude.

It may take you a while to get it right but, just remember, there is no right or wrong way to do it. You just want to create some routine around these cues to train your brain to be resilient and to have fortitude.

Personally, I do this as part of my morning power-up routine (more on that soon). I make sure I take time during the power-up to re-read past experiments, to think about the digital marketing channels we are using and the challenges we have, and to question everything about it. I find it helps me to keep focused on why we are doing what we are doing. Once you start reminding yourself of the incremental gains you have made, the slight setbacks are a lot easier to swallow. This was never more apparent than in my own startup. With Common Ledger (as with any startup), you tend to face more setbacks than steps forward. I had to constantly remind myself why we were doing what we were doing, what the purpose of the company was and how awesome the team was that I worked with. It got me through some difficult times and kept a smile on my face while others around me panicked, stressed, and, in some cases, even fell apart.

ATTRIBUTE 2

CURIOSITY

CURIOSITY

[kyoo r-ee-os-i-tee]
Noun - the desire to learn or know about anything; inquisitiveness
Synonyms - questioning, searching, prying, inquiring mind, thirst for knowledge

Curiosity is a state of active interest. It is where you genuinely and actively want to know more about something. It allows you to fully embrace the unknown, to embrace circumstances and situations that you never previously would have.

Bryant McGill put it best when he said, "Curiosity is one of the great secrets of happiness."

If you are not familiar with Bryant, he is not only a best-selling author, but also the United Nations Appointed 'Global Champion for the Rights of Women and Girls, Gender Equality & Human Rights.' His work has been endorsed by the president of the American Psychological Association (APA), which is my way of saying, "Don't take my word for it; smarter people than me have linked curiosity with happiness."

So why is curiosity such an important mindset to cultivate? To be honest, there are far too many reasons to list here. I am not even going to get started on the fact that the world would be a much better place if people replaced judgement with curiosity. It is far more powerful to try to understand someone different from yourself instead of slapping a label on them and judging them. Okay, deep breath... I almost went down a rabbit hole then.

Okay, so the reason curiosity is important to have in an experimental mindset should be relatively obvious. Most people naturally associate curiosity with experimentation. But there are other important reasons:

Curiosity builds curiosity - Curiosity, like other functions of your brain, is like a muscle. The more you use it, the stronger it gets. It also has the additional benefit of putting the mind in an active and alert state instead of a passive one.

If you ever get the chance (which is my subtle way of saying you should really make the chance), you should read *The Power of Premonitions* by Larry Dossey, MD. In his book, Larry cites studies that have shown that women who regularly read mystery books take themselves out of their familiar routines, which has a positive effect on preserving their mental faculties later in life.

It primes the brain for learning - Your brain is an amazing organ. It often tries to anticipate your needs. This is why a curious mind is more open to learning. When you are curious, your brain expects and anticipates new ideas.

In the study 'States of Curiosity Modulate Hippocampus-Dependent Learning via the Dopaminergic Circuit' conducted for the Center for Neuroscience at the University of California at Davis, it was concluded that people are better at learning information they are curious about. It also concluded that your memory for the incidental material is enhanced during curious states. By the way, if you ever want to look really intelligent, leave a copy of the study on your desk. Most people will only get halfway through the title before concluding that it is too intellectual for them (and therefore, you are, by default, an intellectual).

Additionally, a 2005 report in the *Health Psychology* journal outlined a study where over a thousand patients had seen a correlation between higher levels of curiosity and a decrease in their likelihood of developing hypertension and diabetes. Although this study showed correlation instead of causation, it still shows a very strong suggestion that having a curious mind has additional health benefits.

Basically, having a curious mind will enable you to learn more and retain more of what you have learnt. Not a bad side effect.

Curiosity counters fear - It is pure fact that curiosity helps to allay fear. I need not look further than a situation we had with my son.

We live in Wellington, New Zealand, which means we live in one of the most beautiful cities in the world. We are only a small walk away from native bush walks, beaches, cafes, arts and culture, and more.

However, living in Wellington comes with a few downsides, like the wind and, of course, earthquakes.

I still remember the first big earthquake that my son experienced. It was on one Sunday afternoon when we were all home and, admittedly, it was a particularly scary one. My son was quite shaken by the whole experience, mostly because he felt out of control. I mean, the whole earth just shook violently and there was no warning and all we could do was take cover and hope for the best.

So how did he learn to counter the fear? Simple, we

taught him how to look up the earthquake on Geonet. Geonet is a website that reports all earthquakes in the region and lets you know their magnitude, depth, and where the earthquake is centred. My son immediately became curious. Every time there was an aftershock, instead of cowering in fear, he would run to the computer to look up how big it was. He was fascinated by the fault lines, why the earthquakes were at different depths, how much different a 5.2 earthquake felt from a 7.1, etc. His curiosity had reduced his fear to a mere afterthought.

Curiosity is linked with intelligence -Tthis is an interesting one. In a 2002 study published in the *Journal of Personality and Social Psychology*, researchers had managed to predict (correctly) that toddlers that have higher curiosity levels would grow to have higher IQs than toddlers in the same class that lacked curiosity. I can already hear you muttering, "So what? This may just mean that intelligent people are more curious." This is a very real possibility; however, one thing to note is that curiosity can be cultivated. You can literally train your brain to be curious. So based on this fact, it is not beyond the realms of possibility that training yourself to be curious could have a positive effect on your overall intelligence.

It is also worth pointing out that author and journalist Thomas L. Friedman hypothesised that our brains have more than just Intelligence Quotient (IQ) and Emotional

Quotient (EQ). In fact, Friedman proposed that we also have Curiosity Quotient (CQ) and Passion Quotient (PQ) that combined were greater than IQ.

So according to Friedman, you have the following components:

IQ = Intelligence Quotient = Cognitive and problem-solving ability. Essentially your overall intelligence.

EQ = Emotional Quotient = (the foundation for critical skills) empathy, social skills, anger management, stress tolerance, assertiveness, change tolerance.

CQ = Curiosity Quotient = hunger to want to know more and understand.

PQ = Passion Quotient = your drive and energy to move forward.

And CQ + PQ > IQ

I am not one hundred percent sure I agree with Friedman; however, I do agree that cultivating curiosity is incredibly important and is critical to an experimental mindset.

How do we cultivate curiosity? What can we do to train our brains to be more curious? Here are a few tips I have found that work for me. Try a combination of the following to see what works for you:

ADMIT YOU DON'T HAVE ALL THE ANSWERS

Adults are strange beasts. When we are children, we look at the world with wide-eyed wonder. We have an insatiable thirst for knowledge and don't care what people think... we are going to ask 'why' fifty times in a row until we feel we understand the answer. As adults though, we often put so much pressure on ourselves to look like we know what we are doing. We often fear that others around us may think we are dumb or incompetent if we don't know the answer to an obvious question.

Well, guess what? We don't know everything (in fact, no one does), and that is okay. In fact, it is just fine!

We should just embrace a state of childlike inquisition. Try this: next time you are in the office and someone uses some industry jargon or an acronym that you don't know, instead of nodding like you have a clue, then furiously Googling it afterwards, try asking them what it means. You will often find that others in the room are not aware either and, despite your fears, most people don't judge you for not knowing. If they do judge you for asking questions, you may want to consider that you are in a toxic environment and should possibly look for a new job.

A hilarious example of this happened to me when a presentation was given to a bunch of business leaders (I won't name them for fear of embarrassing them). I wasn't present at the meeting, but I heard that during the presentation there was lots of nodding, agreeing, even clapping at the end. It would be easy to assume that the presentation went well and that everyone in the room was on the same page. However, later that afternoon I received phone calls from a large number of the presentation attendees that wanted me to explain what the presenter was talking about. Each of them had felt like the dumbest person in the room and were too afraid to speak up or ask any questions. The irony is, the presenter had done a terrible job, had used industry jargon, acronyms on acronyms, and had tried to sound as intelligent as possible so that people wouldn't question that fact he too, did not really know what he was doing. It was a shamble of a situation and, fortunately, everyone did eventually build up the courage to ask what it all meant, and the project was scrapped.

QUESTION EVERYTHING

Albert Einstein once wrote: "The important thing is not to stop questioning. Curiosity has its own reason for existing. One cannot help but be in awe when they contemplate the mysteries of eternity, of life, of the marvellous structure of reality."

Life is full of awesome secrets waiting to be unlocked; it is up to you to ask the right questions to unlock them. Believe it or not, questioning everything is a cultivated skill. It is something that you can actively work on. You have to train yourself to be amazed at everyday things. We become so accustomed to life itself that we tend to coast through sometimes. We meander about without noticing how incredible everyday things are around us. Start to discipline yourself to look at things differently. When you look at a roadside curb, have you ever wondered why it is that specific height? Did you even know that there is some research that shows the higher the curb is from the road, the more advanced a city is? Why is that?

Now. I'm not asking you to go out and research curbs. I am more pointing out that asking questions fuels curiosity. The more you ask, the more you want to know. The question "why?" is honestly the most powerful question in the world. Understanding "why" will enable you to have a deeper understanding of the "what" and "how."

Asking questions is also a form of exercise for the mind. Not only will it help to cultivate the curiosity you need for an experimental mindset, but it will also help to keep you sharp and actively searching for insights.

In a digital marketing sense, you can start to ask yourself questions like: "Why do they prefer A to B? Why would someone respond more to a blue banner than a green one? How can this be better? How can I make this an easier experience for consumers?" Ask, ask, ask!

I would also like to point out that there are no stupid questions, only stupid people that are threatened by your simple questions. Okay, I am pretty sure the saying doesn't quite go like that, but you get the drift. Even the smallest of questions can often lead to bigger, more revealing questions. As per the previous section, you don't have to know all the answers, you simply need to be asking the right questions.

SHARPEN YOUR MIND WITH THE MIND OF OTHERS

I am a firm believer in this! To help cultivate your curiosity, you want to make sure you are taking in the right inputs. A lot like your body needs fuel to keep at its peak, your mind needs the right kind of input as well.

Okay, here is a great example. Hopefully, you would have all heard of Leonardo da Vinci (the inventor and artist, not the Teenage Mutant Ninja Turtle). Leo, as his friends called him, was born in 1452 and had one of the most inquisitive minds. Amongst his early artistic endeavours such as painting the Mona Lisa and the Last Supper, Leo was an engineer and avid inventor. In his notebooks, you can find early sketches for a parachute, a giant crossbow, a flying machine, and a mechanical knight (yes, a freakin' robot).

In his notes, you will also find a hidden treasure, something that was an afterthought to most that had seen it. It was a 'to do list.' Have a look at the items on this list (note: this is obviously transcribed from the original Latin):

- [Calculate] the measurement of Milan and its suburbs.

- [Find] a book that treats of Milan and its churches, which is to be had at the stationers on the way to Cordusio.

- [Discover] the measurement of Corte Vecchio (the courtyard in the duke's palace).

- [Discover] the measurement of the Castello (this is palace of the dukes).

- Get the master of arithmetic to show you how to square a triangle.

- Get Messer Fazio (a professor of medicine and law in Pavia) to show you about proportion.

- Get the Brera Friar (at the Benedictine Monastery to Milan) to show you De Ponderibus (a medieval text on mechanics).

- [Talk to] Giannino, the Bombardier, re. the means by which the tower of Ferrara is walled without loopholes (no one really knows what Da Vinci meant by this).

- Ask Benedetto Potinari (a Florentine merchant) by what means they go on ice in Flanders.

- Draw Milan.

- Ask Maestro Antonio how mortars are positioned on bastions by day or night.

- [Examine] the crossbow of Mastro Giannetto.

- Find a master of hydraulics and get him to tell you how to repair a lock, canal, and mill in the Lombard manner.

- [Ask about] the measurement of the sun promised me by Maestro Giovanni Francese.

- Try to get Vitolone (the medieval author of a text on optics), which is in the Library at Pavia, which deals with the mathematic.

The first thing you may notice is Leo's (okay, I admit that

it feels wrong being so informal about such an important historical figure) voracious curiosity. But look a little deeper and you will find a large number of his to-do list involves other people. From picking the brains of Maestro Giovanni Francese or Benedetto Potinari to examining Mastro Giannetto's crossbow. In fact, ten of the fifteen items involve getting information from someone else.

A curious mind is not afraid to ask questions. It is also not afraid to gain knowledge or inspiration from the minds of others.

Now, I'm not suggesting you find fifteenth-century scholars to interrogate or even re-watch *Game of Thrones* so you can remember what a Mastro is. What I am saying is that you need to consume as much as you can. Feed your curiosity beast by reading, reading, and more reading. Watch YouTube videos of people that explain topics you are not normally interested in. Listen to podcasts of people that are solving problems. Let their curiosity sharpen your curiosity. One of the best events I have been to in recent years was a public lecture by Professor Brian Cox. Prof. Cox was explaining how the cosmos works. What was so incredible about the lecture though, was not necessarily the topic (although, come on, space is AWESOME). It was, in fact, the totally infectious curiosity that Prof. Brian and all of the great minds that he talked about had. I took my son with me to the event and the two of us came away with our minds blown and a passion to investigate further, a passion to understand things. If we refer back to the previous analogy of curiosity being like a muscle, then coming away from the lecture was akin to a runner's high. We did not want to stop being curious.

TREAT IT AS A KEYSTONE HABIT

We all know what habits are, for good and for bad. For example, a good habit I have managed to cultivate over the past year is to walk as often as possible. My wife and I treat walking as a time for us to catch up as well as to get some fresh air. We set a target to walk at least 25Km a week in winter and 50Km a week in summer. This habit has helped me to lose over 16Kg, as well as strengthen what was already an awesome relationship. On the flip side, I also have a bad habit of biting my nails, something that, despite trying, I cannot seem to break.

Basically, habits are those acquired behaviours that we form from regularly following a routine until it becomes involuntary.

What is a keystone habit then? Glad you asked. From what I can tell, the concept of keystone habits originated in the must-read book *The Power of Habit* by Charles Duhigg. The concept of a keystone habit is that it is a habit that can be correlated with other good habits.

Let me try to explain this with a couple of examples and then try to explain why we should focus on trying to create curiosity as not only a habitual behaviour but as a keystone habit.

First, let's look at an obvious negative example of a keystone habit, and that is drugs. My talented wife Leanne is an addictions counselor and has seen firsthand the ripple effect that a drug habit has on the rest of an individual's life. It causes bad decisions and other behaviours that become habitual. Some become habitual liars to try and hide their behaviour from their loved ones, others will demonstrate self-destructive patterns with their relationships. It forms a negative spiral that all stems from one keystone habit.

Let's have a look at a more positive example of a keystone habit. In this case, I will use my own example of my power-up routine. If I go back over ten years ago, I would start the day feeling aimless and cluttered. I would find mornings stressful, as I often had a lot to do to prepare for the day (and get the kids ready for school, etc), yet I always found I was chasing my tail. Now, I can hear you saying to yourself, "Well, Vince, that is not so bad, as most of us have too little time to achieve what we need to in the mornings, and we do our best in the chaos" (at least, I hope it is your voice saying that; otherwise, I may be going slightly mad here). You are right. Most people do have too little time to get things done in the mornings, but to put things in context for you, I am a little different. Since I was little I have only ever needed a very small amount of sleep. Essentially, I only sleep four hours a night and, as such, I get up at 3 a.m. every morning. So now you can start to understand why I was getting so frustrated. I had more time than most and definitely more time than needed to be able to start my day right and get everything I needed to do.

So, enter my power-up routine. I wish I could remember where I came up with the concept, as I am certain I just stole the idea from someone or something that I read one day, but the idea was to structure my time. I wanted to ensure that my day started in a productive way and that I would no longer feel like I was chasing my tail. I feel I need to clarify here that chasing my tail is just a saying. I do not, nor have I ever had a tail in my life. Although, in saying that, once the technology is available, I would not say no to a mechanical prehensile tail. It would be so handy. Anyway, I digress.

So back to this power-up routine. I discovered that having a structure in my morning made me feel in control and had a flow-on effect on how I faced the day. So, I started to write down what I wanted to achieve each morning. I used the concept of Kaizen (continuous improvement) to work out what I should do and break it into bite-sized chunks. I started by taking 30 minutes to do some upskilling by reading some white papers, articles, blogs, or books. Then each week I would add a new task to the power-up routine.

I discovered that the more I did this, the better I felt. The more I did it, the better the rest of my habits became. Instead of spending 30 minutes in the office having a coffee and procrastinating starting the day, I would turn up to the office obnoxiously positive and energetic. I also evolved the power-up routine over time until it now looks like this:

- 30 minutes reading to upskill
- 30 minutes researching new trends or info that is relevant to the digital marketing industry
- 30 minutes of writing
- 15 minutes of trying to actively relax, usually doing breathing exercises or contemplating complex algorithms
- 15 minutes planning my day (I love writing lists, so this is super handy)
- 15 minutes having coffee and breakfast (don't judge me, I am a ridiculously quick eater)
- 15 minutes shower, shave, etc.
- 30 minutes tidying up the house (if needed) and getting a coffee ready so that when my awesome wife Leanne wakes up there is a fresh cup waiting

for her

I would love to say that I achieved this every morning, but sometimes things happen to interrupt the routine. However, most days I would do a fair chunk of it.

Bringing this all back to how it relates to curiosity, you can see from both the positive and negative habits above (power-up routines vs drugs) that habits have a ripple effect or chain reaction that affect other habits. That chain reaction is what makes them a keystone habit. Curiosity, if cultivated, is no different. If you actively work on being more curious, there are significant flow-on effects. You will face the day with a positive outlook and you will start to increase your happiness, which will inevitably lead to better habits throughout the day.

It can be hard to wrap our heads around the importance of curiosity, but I genuinely believe it makes us happier, more positive, and, let's face it, better human beings. Curiosity is a key component in empathy.

I wish I had more time to go into curiosity, but we have so much more to cover in the book. Long story short... be curious!!!

ATTRIBUTE 3

CONFIDENCE

CONFIDENCE

[kon-fi-duh ns]

Noun - belief in oneself and one's powers or abilities; self-confidence; self-reliance; assurance

Synonyms - determination, courage, certainty, fearlessness, resolution, sureness

So far, we have covered Fortitude and Curiosity as key elements that you will need to ensure you have the right mindset for experimentation – an "experimental mindset" if you will. So now let's have a look at the next key – 'confidence' – and why it is such an important component of having that experimental mindset. What advantages does confidence bring? How can it help you to stay positive? How does it keep you focused? First up though, let's have a look at what confidence is and why it is so important.

I think at this point we need to start by highlighting what confidence isn't. It isn't unmerited arrogance. Confidence is not mindless ignorance either. No, confidence has a huge element of self-awareness about it. It is a belief in your own capabilities, even if you are treading in unfamiliar territory. You know yourself well enough to understand that you are capable of succeeding. It is understanding your own experience, skills, and capabilities, and not putting unnecessary pressure on yourself. In fact, if you think about it, confidence can be the antithesis of fear and, as we know, fear is the enemy of good decision making.

Let me give you two examples to help you understand what confidence is and isn't.

FALSE CONFIDENCE

Imagine I am at a sporting event (yes, I know that is a stretch, but let's just picture it for a moment). Say, for example, I am at a rugby match and one of the players gets injured. They don't have enough players to continue playing, so they ask for a volunteer from the crowd (yes, I know this is a very unlikely scenario, but hey, we just pictured me at a sporting event, so weirder things have happened). I eagerly put my hand up and think to myself, "I've seen rugby on TV, how hard can it be?" Now let's be clear, I haven't been trained or coached. In fact, I barely even know the rules. This will not stop me though; I believe in myself and am exuding confidence. This is not confidence at all. In fact, there is only one way this ends, with me humiliating myself and leaving the field on a stretcher. Confidence is not blind faith in oneself. It is an awareness of our own capabilities, our own strengths and weaknesses. Once you know yourself, you can and should back yourself. However, in this sports scenario, I am fooling myself. I am in no way gifted with any ability to catch a ball, and running and I don't really see eye to eye. So now let's look at another scenario.

TRUE CONFIDENCE

This is a hard one to articulate, but I will try by illustrating a real-life scenario that happened to me recently. I received a voicemail from an event organiser asking if I could speak at an event on Artificial Intelligence. I was about to call him back to decline when I stopped and took stock. On one hand, I have a principle that I do not speak on topics that I cannot add value to. On the other hand, I love public speaking (okay, I admit it, I really just love being the centre of attention). So I looked at who is going to be at the event and it turns out it will be a mix of data scientists, artificial intelligence experts and enthusiasts, and business leaders who are no doubt working on A.I. projects. Then I looked at myself. What experience do I have in A.I.? Well, I am working on some projects and have tinkered with Natural Language Processing at home (yes, I lead a very geeky life). However, in no way am I an expert. The good thing is that I mentioned this to a colleague of mine named Nathan. He challenged me on a particular point. He pointed out that part of the project I was working on involved a large amount of research into artificial intelligence (and I am one of those weird geeky types that also researches technology for fun). I had looked into what had worked and what hadn't, why projects in A.I. succeeded and why they failed. I had met with many (and I do mean many) experts on the topic to discuss various approaches, all of which had helped me to formulate an approach to A.I. as it relates to interaction with the public. Nathan pointed out that I had a unique approach to this and that it could be valuable to a room full of developers and scientists. So I called them back and said yes.

I was so glad I did the event. I met some awesome people and had a lot of positive feedback on my approach to A.I.-based projects. You see, this is true confidence. Knowing yourself well enough (even after being prompted) to know that you can add value to the audience. It was a belief in my own experience and abilities to know that I did not have to have all of the answers. In fact, I was completely up front with the crowd and said, "Hands up if you are a Machine

Learning Engineer. Any Data Scientists? Any Artificial Intelligence experts? Well I am none of these." If any curly questions came up, I was completely transparent about the fact that I did not have the answer. I could then use the opportunity to talk them through how I would go about getting the answers if I needed to. We had great feedback from the session, and a number of the specialists had followed up with me afterwards to sense check their own approaches.

So why is this 'True Confidence' and not 'False Confidence'? It all comes down to me understanding myself and understanding my own strengths and weaknesses. It is me having a good understanding of what I bring to the table and then backing myself to be able to deliver it. Self-doubt is a killer that often stops us from ever trying or even starting something.

I remember when I was a lot younger and I was going to a business breakfast. I was surrounded by experienced business people in expensive-looking suits (I have no idea if they were expensive or not; this was just how it seemed to me at the time). The speaker was the Oceanic sales rep for Adobe. Now, full disclosure, at the time I was both a fully-fledged Adobe fanboy (a fact that to date has not changed) AND I felt like I did not deserve to be there. I was young, inexperienced, and surrounded by what I had perceived as success. The speaker was amazing, he commanded presence on stage, and effortlessly answered every question. It was then that the unthinkable happened. The speaker came and joined us at our table. What would I say? How could I look like I deserved to be there? I knew I had to ask a question. I knew it had to be a good one. I nervously asked the best question I could think of: "At what point did you know you had made it?" I looked at the faces of the rest of the table and realised that this was not a good question at all; what an incredibly naive thing to ask. As I started to feel embarrassed by what had just come out of my mouth, his answer surprised me. He looked me right in the eye and said, "Want to know my secret?" I nodded politely while my anticipation levels started to spike. Could this mean I was about to get the secret to success? Will he have a magic formula that would make me instantly have as much knowledge as everyone else in the room seemed to have? He looked me in the eye again and started to tell me about his morning routine. I grabbed my paper and pen and started to capture notes. There was no way I wanted to miss any of this. I wanted to absorb every gem, every tip that came out of his mouth.

"Every morning I go through a routine. I fill the sink with cold water. I splash the water all over my face…" This was gold, and I wrote down each step. "I then look at myself in the mirror and say to myself, 'Today is the day they find out you are a fraud!'" I was speechless. I am sure the rest of the table were as well, but I was so engrossed in the moment, I do not even remember them at all.

"Fraud," I murmered.

"Yeah, fraud."

Then I realised... wait a minute... you know what you are doing... you are good at this! That is when I got one of the best pieces of advice in my career: "I always feel like a fraud, like I don't belong there, like I don't deserve to sit at the table with everyone else. Most people do!"

This floored me. Not only to hear that one of the people I look up to felt the same way that I did, but that most people also felt the same way. I looked around the room and saw everyone in a new light. Suddenly everyone no longer looked as intimidating as before; suddenly everyone looked as vulnerable as I was feeling. This gave me a new perspective. This speaker was one of the most confident people I had ever seen, yet he constantly battled with not feeling worthy. His words have stuck with me to this day. One point in particular: the part where he reminded himself that he knows what he is doing. The part where he reminded himself that he was good at this.

Back then there did not seem to be a name for this phenomenon. These days we know it as imposter syndrome, that feeling that holds us back because we do not feel like we deserve success or to sit at the table with everyone else. The secret to confidence was in fact wrapped up in what he told me. The fact that, despite how he felt, he still reminded himself that he knew what he was doing and that he backed himself. That amazing public speaker that answered questions so effortlessly had built his confidence by both understanding his strengths (and weaknesses), and then, despite a crippling feeling of unworthiness, still put himself forward and said yes to opportunities.

The other thing that fascinated me about this story was the fact that most people seem to have the same lack of self-belief. I found this interesting because it meant that I should not judge myself on how I perceive others to be (keyword there is 'perceive'). We have no idea what other people think and feel. We have no idea what they are going through and whether they believe in themselves or not. The only thing we can really measure ourselves against is... well, ourselves. You see, confidence is not necessarily about knowing answers to tough situations or questions, it is just having an understanding that we have the ability to be able to find those answers. That we can back ourselves to know that whatever is put in front of us, we have the skills and experience to be able to work through it.

So, if confidence is about understanding our strengths and weaknesses, why is confidence so important to an experimental mindset then? Great question! There are three things I know about confidence:

Confidence is contagious. Famous American football player and coach Vince Lombardi once quipped, "Confidence is contagious, so is lack of confidence." This is widely recognised in the psychology industry. In fact, there have been so many studies on how emotions affect people around you that psychologists have even given it its own name: "Emotional Contagion" (or EC). It is used to describe the fact that we tend to mimic the emotional expressions of others. Just look at how a negative person can bring down the mood of an entire team. Or how an overly bubbly person can seem to put a smile on the face of those they interact with. Similarly, confidence creates a positive energy that can be contagious. Remember what we said at the beginning of the Experimental Mindset section of this book: "It is you who will determine how well your experimental methodology is adopted by your team and the wider company." You are the evangelist for experimentation, and the more confident energy you display, the more confidence the team and the company will have in this approach.

People are attracted to confidence. Now before you get too excited, I am not saying that you having confidence in your new experimental approach will help to find you a soul mate (you never know though, stranger things have happened). What I am saying is that the key to success for experimentation is getting the buy-in from the rest of the business. Think of PowerStorm Sessions: they only work when people have bought into the process and are engaged. Confidence has an attractive quality to it. People are naturally attracted to confidence and, as such, will want to be a part of what you are selling (in case I wasn't clear, you are selling the experimental approach here). What we are effectively saying here is that you need to rise to be a leader, a leader in driving this change. To quote another famous American football player and coach (who would have thought I would quote sporting personalities... will wonders never cease?) Tom Landry, "Leadership is a matter of having people look at you and gain confidence, seeing how you react. If you're in control, they're in control."

The third thing I know is that confidence is a skill. In a paper published in *Psychology Today*, Erika Casriel pointed out that the most socially confident people deliberately learn specific skills. She points out that we often look at confident individuals and assume they were born that way. In fact, confidence is a skill, and skills can be trained and cultivated. I guess what I am trying to say here is that there is good news. We can ALL train to be confident, we just need to practice and work at it.

There are also a number of techniques to try to increase our self-confidence, including:

Dressing better - Have you ever noticed how good you feel when you wear new clothes or dress for a job interview? Ever felt that buzz when you are getting ready to go to a ball or a gala? Dressing better has an effect on our mental state. If you are a corporate casual kind of person, maybe think about stepping it up half a notch? If you come to work in

154

jeans and a T-shirt, maybe try wearing shirts. It is up to you. Play around with it and see how you feel.

Power poses - This is a discredited hypothesis by Dana Carney, Amy Cuddy, and Andy Yap that claims having a powerful posture can help with your confidence. "Okay, Vince, if this is discredited, then why include it?" Simple, it may be now considered pseudoscience, but the act of trying something new puts us in a different mental state (refer to the chapters on curiosity). Give it a shot as a way to help try to trigger your brain to feel confidence. Even though the pose itself may not work, the fact is we are trying to tell our brain, "I want to feel confident right now." At the very least, you will have some fun practising standing like Superman.

Affirmations - I have made affirmations part of my morning power-up routine now. This is the act of speaking positive statements about yourself out loud. It is about being in conscious control of your thoughts. Try telling yourself every morning, "I have a right to be at the table with everyone else." You will be surprised at the power of your own words. The more you affirm positive (and realistic) statements such as, "I know what I am doing" and "I bring a lot to the table," the more your brain starts to accept them as a truth. There is a huge amount of studies behind positive affirmations that we don't have time to go into here (remember, I promised to keep us on track). Just give it a go and you will see what I mean. Oh, and don't worry, everyone feels silly the first time they try affirmations... that is quite normal. You will quickly get used to it.

Train your vocabulary - This one takes a lot of practice, but it is absolutely vital in training confidence. Start to observe your vocabulary in different situations. When someone asks if you can solve an issue or a problem, how do you reply? Do you immediately start to highlight why it may not be possible? Do you respond with self-doubt or negativity? Try something different. Try responding with, "Not a problem, leave that with me." Say it with confidence (even if you are not feeling it at the time). Remember, you wouldn't be where you are if you did not know a thing or two.

Read more - In reality, this is a piece of advice I can put against every point in this book. Reading helps to expand our thinking, to gain perspective. Try reading books like *The Subtle Art of Not Giving a F*CK* by Mark Manson. These kinds of books help to understand that life is short, that you need to selectively choose what you want to care (or give a f*ck) about. You need to care about what is true, immediate, and important to you. Treat these things as your priorities. Once you establish what your priorities and goals are, you can make the choice to not worry about what others think. Have confidence.

ATTRIBUTE 4

OPEN-MINDED-NESS

OPEN-MINDED-NESS

[oh-puh n-mahyn-did-ness]

Adjective - having or showing a mind receptive to new ideas or arguments. Unprejudiced; unbigoted; unbiased; impartial.

Synonyms - unbiased, unprejudiced, prejudice-free, accepting, non-partisan, neutral, non-aligned, non-judgemental, non-discriminatory

First of all, yes, I am aware that the actual title of this section should be open-minded. However, the fact that I made the grammar nazis of you stop and pay attention is exactly why I call this Open-minded-ness. To be fair, a true grammar nazi would have stopped reading this book ages ago with my colorful and warped use of basic English.

Anyway, I digress. Alongside Fortitude, Curiosity, and

Confidence, Open-minded-ness is a critical element to ensuring you have the right mindset for experimentation, or, as we are calling it, an "experimental mindset."

So why is keeping an open mind so important? Glad you asked. Essentially, this is the chapter where we reference one of my favorite topics: 'Cognitive Bias.' Or, as I like to put it, your brain's inability to accurately process and analyse data.

Dedicating an entire book to gleaning insights through experimentation is going to be next to useless if we do not have the ability (through our own faulty wiring) to be able to accurately analyse and draw conclusions on the data at hand.

So this part of the experimental mindset is designed to help you to understand how your brain tries to misinterpret information through shortcuts known as cognitive biases. Then you, by understanding these biases, can eliminate the power that it has over you.

So first up, what exactly is a cognitive bias?

The definition of cognitive bias is a 'deviation from rationality in judgment.' Essentially, it is a shortcut that our brain takes to speed up decision making, something that is particularly important when a decision requires timeliness more than accuracy. It is also a way for our brain to conserve energy. You have to remember that this supercomputer we call a brain takes a lot of energy to process the one exaFLOP it needs to do daily (ExaFLOP is a very geeky way of saying one billion billion calculations per second). By reducing this energy, your brain can process more important functions, like remembering to breathe or putting pants on before going to work.

Let me give you an exaggerated example to help understand why we take these shortcuts (or biases). Imagine for a moment you are walking along at night and come across someone who does not speak your language and is aggressively yelling at you while holding a knife. Think about this for a moment. There would be very few of us who haven't already thought in our minds "run" as we picture the scenario.

Let us take a step back though and look at what the brain has to process in order to accurately analyse the situation at hand. To do this, let us look at each of the elements in the story:

Yelling - One of the things our brain has to analyse is why this man is standing in front of us with a raised voice. Is it just that his language is jarring to me and I am misinterpreting it as aggressive? Is he merely being passionately loud? Is he trying to talk to someone way behind me? Analysing this is made complex by the fact that we do not understand the language that he is speaking. You may not be consciously aware of this, but our brains are wired to think of a raised voice as aggressive behaviour.

The man - We then have to assess the man walking towards us. Is he threatening? What does he want? Why is he walking towards me? Does the way he is walking indicate aggression? Why on earth is he wearing that top with those pants?

The knife - The obvious question here is why is a man standing in front of me carrying a knife? Is he threatening me? Is he giving me the knife as a gift? Is he showing me the quality of a knife he has just sharpened? Does he want to prepare some food for me? I know this sounds ridiculous, but if we did not use our bias, which helps our brain go "in action movies, knife equals danger," then we may just end up in the emergency room trying not to bleed out.

It is an over-exaggerated example, but it helps to make the point that in a situation that is time critical (i.e., an imminent threat), our brains have to process the information as efficiently as possible. So our previous understandings, experiences, and world views kick in and form a cognitive bias to help speed up the analysis.

So how does this apply to chasing insights through the results from our experimentation? Good question. You see, our brain takes these shortcuts for good and for bad. For example, our brain is hardwired to release dopamine (a chemical that our neurons release) when we anticipate a reward (or success). This can mean that our brain automatically looks at results to try and find success where there may be none. Dopamine is a powerful motivator. Just look at high-reward games like Candy Crush (or my personal addiction, Toy Blast), where you are rewarded with a new level every time you complete the menial task of matching colors. The feeling you get when you achieve something – in this case, unlocking the new level – results in wasting many hours on a game that achieves nothing.

My goal here is to run through the basic categories of cognitive bias and some of the more pertinent examples to help you to be aware of them. Trust me, the more you are aware of them, the more you will start to ask yourself the hard questions when looking for insights.

Let's have a look at the four main groupings of cognitive bias:

1. *Biases based on having too much information* – This is where we pay attention to things that are already primed in our thoughts and memories. Often our brains are looking at all of the stored information that we have, then we process and analyse information with a lens to validate the large quantum of data that is already in our memories.

2. ***Biases that arise from not enough meaning*** – This is where our brain tries to analyse information without understanding context. You will find that things like stereotyping come into play here. Our brain also up-weights information we are familiar with over the unfamiliar and therefore relies solely on the limited information we have from our own experience.

3. ***Biases that are based on the limitation of our memory (or how we remember)*** – Ever relay a past story to someone else that was there, only to find that (despite how vividly we remember) we remembered it in the wrong location? Or that someone you thought was present was not? We will go through this a little more shortly, but our brains edit memories after the fact. We cannot rely on our own past experiences when we attempt to analyse our own information.

4. ***Biases based on the brains requirement to act fast*** – as per the knife example previously, our brains sometimes have to react rapidly. With this in mind, we tend to favour the simple options over the more complex. We also resist change when we have to move fast (the simple and familiar are easier to process).

Hopefully that has helped you to understand the main

groupings of cognitive bias, and now I want to highlight some of the more relevant biases that are likely to encounter (or display). Let's have a look at twelve different cognitive biases that you are likely to come across in your daily lives as marketers trying to chase insights. Now if any of you have Obsessive Compulsive Disorder (OCD), you may be wondering why I am highlighting twelve and not a nice round number like ten. Well, that is simply because I chose the ten I thought were most relevant to highlight and then remembered two fun ones that I wanted to share with you. So, based on simple math, 10 + 2 = 12. Besides, if we were to try to analyse all of the cognitive biases that have been identified, we would be here a while. Depending on who you ask, there can be over 100 different biases. When you read the biases below, you will notice that each one is only touched on very lightly. That is because I want you to go away and look into each of the biases as you work through debiasing (more on that shortly).

Let's have a look at these in no particular order:

Anchoring bias - This is where we have a natural habit of relying on "anchors" when making decisions. These are single pieces of information or traits (often the first piece of information we have on that specific subject).

Availability heuristic - This is where we tend to put too much credibility on the likelihood of events that have a greater "availability" in our memory. This can also be influenced by how emotionally charged the memories are.

Confirmation bias - This is by far one of the most common biases with marketers. Basically, it is when we process and analyse information in such a way that it confirms our own preconceptions. Let's face it, we all want that rush of winning, so our brains focus on information and memories that prove we are right.

Information bias - This is where we look for information, even when it cannot affect any action. We have a tendency to do this when we lack confidence or clarity. There is a part of our brain that immediately thinks more information is better. For a good example of this, refer to any social media marketer's analysis of a campaign. How many vanity metrics can we pack into one dashboard or report that have no relation to how well the campaign is performing?

Base rate fallacy - This is where we look at things in too much isolation. It is our tendency to ignore general or generic information (base rate information) and only focus on information that is connected with what we are trying to prove.

Clustering illusion - This is also far too common with marketers. It is where we overestimate small runs of data. We look at the information in clusters rather than as a whole and identify small streaks (sometimes referred to as phantom patterns). You see this in play when analysing experiments that have data with a high amount of volatility. The minute we see a spike towards improvement, we mentally assume the experiment a success despite the fact that there is a trend towards the negative overall.

Expectation bias - Sometimes referred to as expectancy bias. This is very similar to confirmation bias with the main difference being that confirmation bias focuses only on info that agrees with your preconceived ideas, whereas expectation bias affects the outcome based on your own expectations. It is the tendency to discard or down-weight data that differs from your expectations. Again, this is one that is far too common in marketing.

Observer-expectancy effect - You particularly see this one at play during focus groups or consumer research. Essentially, it is where the researcher inadvertently manipulates the participants due to having a expectation of a result. If you ever hear a researcher (or yourself) say anything along the lines of, "Well, obviously you would all choose the blue pill... explain why," chances are, they did not want the blue pill, but you have now put the thought in their head that they would have chosen it.

Post-purchase rationalization - This one usually relates to post-purchase behaviour (e.g., you have just purchased a new pair of headphones and you settled for a lower quality than you wanted because it was easier to order them. Now you are listening to music trying to convince yourself that it does sound as good as the new Audio Technicas... sigh.) My purchase regrets aside, this can outwork itself when reviewing an experiment. You make a number of decisions to implement a hypothesis test and occasionally our brains do not want to admit we made a bad decision, so we analyse the results of a campaign to justify the decisions made.

Framing effect - This is where the way we frame results can affect our analysis of the outcome. If we describe things in a positive frame, our brains tend to avoid looking for risks or negative factors in the analysis. The opposite is true if it is described or positioned in a negative frame. We tend to look for the risks and seek out the negative (and positive) factors. Essentially, it is using a too-narrow approach and description of the situation or issue that pre-determines the outcome.

And now the two bonus ones I mentioned:

Hawthorne effect - This one is the bane of researchers. It is effectively where an individual that is participating in a piece of research modifies their behaviour because they know they are being observed. You see this a lot in start-ups. If you were to walk up to individuals and describe your service, then ask them if they would pay for it, often they say they will.

However, once left to their own devices, they have very little motivation to go through with signing up for your service. In start-ups, we call it the penny gap. In research, it is the annoying fact that an experiment can show a positive result, yet when you roll the experiment into everyday activity, the positive gains you noticed cannot be replicated.

Dunning-Kruger effect - This is where we mistakenly assess our own cognitive abilities as greater than they actually are. It is a catchall for those of us who get complacent and think we have this whole open-minded-ness sorted. "I don't need to think too much about my biases, as I am an expert in keeping an open mind during analysis." We need to actively question our own cognitive abilities! We need to constantly ask how our own thinking and behaviour affect the outcome or analysis of an experiment.

So how do we reduce the effect of cognitive bias? Are we already doomed? Should we just give up now and go home?

Relax, there is a simple way to deal with the negative effects of cognitive bias. In fact, studies from the likes of Gigerenzer in 1996 and Haselton in 2005 came to an interesting conclusion. They determined that the direction and content of cognitive biases are not "arbitrary." What this basically means is that you can actually control cognitive bias through a technique called "debiasing" (sometimes called cognitive bias mitigation).

DEBIASING

Now let us have a quick look at debiasing. Despite what it sounds like, debiasing is not something the FBI have to take cult survivors through. It is in fact a rather simple technique for reducing the effect of bias on our judgment and decision making. Traditionally, it is broken into three main methods: Incentives, Nudges, and Training; however, I am not going to go fully into these methods, as that will take us off track and, if I am honest, 'Incentives' and 'Nudges' do not really apply when applying debiasing to understanding experiment results (at least not when it comes to digital marketing). Instead I am going to focus on the third method for debiasing, which is 'Training.' In fact, I would even like to introduce a new part to this method; let's call it 'Conscious Questioning.'

Let me explain. The traditional 'Training' method of debiasing involves a number of techniques, including:

- Teaching the researchers to consider the alternative. Basically, getting them to think of a plausible alternative reason for the result.

- Providing individual feedback to the researcher to highlight any observed bias. This is simply highlighting their shortcomings to help them learn.

- Encouraging the researcher to take the perspective of the user. Often, researchers can get so caught up in their own bias that they do not consider that a human being (as weird and wonderful as they are) is on the other end of the experiment.

- Encouraging the researcher to consider the consequences of their findings on users. In other words, what result would your conclusion have on a consumer or customer?

You may have already noticed this, but each of these techniques involves one common thread, which is getting the researcher to actively think about the decisions they are making (or in our case, the insights they are extracting from the experiment). Like most things in life, the more we know about something, the more we can negate the effect it has on us.

"So, what does this mean, Vince? Do we all need to enroll in a training course for debiasing? Do we need to travel to the Himalayas to apprentice under a debiasing guru?" Nope, it is actually a lot simpler than that. Just follow the four steps below and you will be well on your way to mitigating any of your inbuilt biases.

STEP ONE - LEARN

This is the training part of the 'Training' method. The good news is, the fact that you are this far through this chapter means you are already well on your way. The goal of this step is to understand as much as you can about cognitive bias and how it may affect you. Go through the ones I have listed earlier in this chapter. Try to get your brain around why each of these cognitive biases exist and how they affect your decision making. Don't stop there though; there are many books, papers, and articles on cognitive bias. Remember, knowledge is power, and reading up on these biases is one of your best weapons in defeating them.

STEP TWO - PAUSE

Most cognitive bias occurs due to our brain's habit of "automatic processing." This is our brain's way of conserving energy. If you can make decisions on auto-pilot (basically without having to use much brain power), then you create efficiencies. That is why this step is designed to force you to take a moment and use the concept of "controlled processing." That is, to deliberately force yourself to consider a number of factors before determining an outcome or extracting an insight.

STEP THREE - ASK

So now you know about some of the different biases and you have even taken a moment to pause so your brain doesn't try to process the results of an experiment on auto-pilot... what now? Well, now is the step I like to call "Conscious Questioning." It is forcing the brain to look at different aspects of the experiment through different lenses. It is asking yourself the right questions to get your brain to ignore a bias and make decisions off of conscious thought. So how do we do this? Easy! When you have paused in the previous step, you can use the pause to ask some questions of yourself. Personally, I like to look at the biases that affect me most, or the ones that are more relevant to the current situation, and ask myself some hard questions. Let me give you an example.

Let's pretend I am running an experimental lead generation campaign and want to know if the results are showing positive compared to previous campaigns. Now the particularly perceptive amongst you may have already seen the problem that has just occurred: that's right, based on the way I described the example, there is a risk that I am being affected by either Confirmation Bias or Expectation Bias. Basically, the fact that I want to see if it is a positive result may mean I have gone in expecting that it has. So what do I do? Simple, I have already understood the biases that may affect me and I have just paused to ensure I am using controlled processing. Now I want to ask some questions of myself.

Here is a small selection of some of the questions I often ask:

- What is my expectation for the experiment?

- Am I okay with disproving my hypothesis?

- What is my sample size?

- What are my baseline results?

- What external factors could have affected the results?

- Am I inadvertently affecting the outcome of the experiment in any way?

STEP FOUR - REPEAT

This one is going to sound particularly obvious, but the concept of open-minded-ness is not a set and forget process or, for that matter, something you can achieve with learning about a process once before being cured. This is an ongoing process, something that you need to actively work towards and continue to challenge yourself on. Make this process part of your conscious thought process every time you are trying to analyse results from an experiment. You owe it to yourself.

There you have it. Not only do you now understand the

concept of open-minded-ness, you should now have a good understanding of what it takes to have the right mindset to successfully implement an experimentational approach to digital marketing (or any form of marketing, for that matter).

Now before we wrap all of this up into a neat bow and get onto the last part of this book, I quickly want to cover something else that you will find invaluable when it comes to an experimental approach. That something is your budget.

So, let us have a look at...

THE
EXPERIMENTAL
BUDGET

THE EXPERIMENTAL BUDGET

I have taken the methodology and mindset of experimentation to a ridiculous amount of marketing professionals and, without a doubt, the most common response is, "This sounds amazing, but how do I find the budget to implement it?" Or, "I will never get this past our Chief Financial Officer."

I find that, every time, I have to take them through the same conversation. First, I debunk the theory that the CFO will oppose this. In fact, in my experience, CFOs or any finance types absolutely love having something that has its own framework of evaluation built in. Not only are you able to quantify any results that you see, but you do so in a test and learn framework, which means you are able to prove the value of an experiment without having to commit large suitcases full of cash.

The next part of the conversation is always around creating the concept of an experimental budget. And before you ask, no, this does not mean you are playing around with using various forms of currency to pay for a marketing campaign (although the thought of paying an agency to produce a campaign using 'Chickens' does intrigue me).

Basically, what I am trying to say is that you can build experimentation into your budget planning.

So let's have a look at three things you could either do or consider.

THE RULE OF 90/10

This is something we implemented a while back that we found paid dividends on dividends on even more dividends.

Traditionally, any budget set aside to run an experiment is treated in one of two ways.

First, it is treated as either a buffer or slush budget. Trust me when I tell you, these two words need to be removed from your vocabulary, mainly because using those terms in front of a CFO will lose you a substantial amount of credibility. The other reason to remove them from your vocabulary is due to the fact that you will mentally position the budget (and therefore the experiment) as optional or negotiable. When you build experimentation into your budget, you treat it as important as your standard campaigns or media. Remember, experimentation can give you a chance to discover profitable (and otherwise unknown) channels.

The second way we treat that pool of money set aside to run an experiment is that it is treated as a program of work that needs to stack up against profitability. The problem with this (which I am sure you have already picked up on now that you have open-minded-ness) is that this approach will potentially obscure your results. Remember, you are not chasing the win, you are chasing the insights. How do you quantify insights? How do you try to calculate the profitability of something that may have a positive effect on your bottom line further down the track?

This is where the 90/10 rule comes into play. Basically, we build the experimentation into the budget lines themselves. For example, if you have set aside a monthly budget for paid search, ensure the forecasted cost will only be 90% of your expense for that channel. The additional 10% is set aside for running experiments on paid search. You can use it to test new search terms, new copy, or new offers.

The same principle goes for display, social media, any web builds you have scheduled, and even your creative. Just think, 10% of your creative expense can be to test new media types, B versions of display ads to A/B test against, new UX designs, etc.

Having this discipline gives you a strategic advantage and means you are actively and consciously looking for ways to spend the experimental budget. This will keep you disciplined in experimental methodology. It's a win win!

SELL THE FULL STORY

The other thing I get people to consider when they put the CFO lens over experimentation is how to sell the whole story. This is an absolutely vital part of the process and not just for your CFO, but also all of your senior management. You NEED to bring them on the journey with you. A huge part of implementing an experimental framework is you telling stories. Your job is to become the biggest evangelist for experimentation. You need to re-explain the process as often as people will continue to listen. You also need to give visibility of the progress and take the time to explain the results (and why they are so important).

You also need to talk them through the different aspects of the process. Let me give you a good example. I remember going to our head of Finance to give him the invoice for some qualitative consumer research we had done. You could immediately see his eyes roll and his butt cheeks clench as he leaned forward to see how much this had cost. Remember, those in Finance completely understand the need for consumer feedback and research; however, they also see how much it costs (and those of you that have conducted this type of research know it is not cheap). But this is where the story took a turn. I looked at the head of Finance's face and a miracle happened. His mouth made a creaking noise as it curled up at the sides. Our CFO was smiling!

What caused this smile? Well, remember how we explained some of the different techniques you can employ when implementing the C.H.A.S.E.R. method? We had used Coffee Line Tests to talk some of the general public through aspects of our proposed designs for an online form. We had incredible feedback from the participants that completely reshaped our approach. And the costs? Only $85 for a bunch of coffees. Now that is something that anyone in Finance can get behind.

Remember, take them on the journey and they will feel like they are part of the process. It is a lot easier for them to get their heads around the 10% set aside for experimentation when they can clearly see the value you are gaining from it.

INCLUDE INSIGHTS AS PART OF YOUR ROI

All of us at some point will have to justify the Return on Investment (ROI) for any work that we do. It makes sense, right?! You cannot sustain a business if the costs, and the return on those costs, do not stack up. In fact, I am pretty confident that most of you reading this have had to write up Post-Implementation Reports (or PIRs) for campaigns or programs at work. If you have, you will know the stress of trying to show the true value of a campaign or project. If you haven't done a PIR report before (or you are reading this and saying to yourself, "What the hell are you on about, Vinny?"), do not stress; it is just an evaluation of the work to assess if the objectives were met.

Essentially, the trick here is to simply add the insights as part of your evaluation on the ROI. Or, in other words, you want to ensure that people (yourself included) understand the intangible value that is gained from running an experiment.

So how do we do this? Well, the good news is that you are already doing this as part of the C.H.A.S.E.R. method. Remember the A (Agenda) part of the process? Remember how we kept an area of the Agenda for you to write up both the results and the insights you gained from it? In the words of the immortal Harry Houdini, "Ta Daaa" (okay, maybe don't quote me on the source of that one).

Now, you may be wondering why I have even included this point, considering you are already doing it. Well, one thing I discovered very early in my experimentation journey was that it is easy to forget the value of an insight when you are explaining (or in some cases trying to justify) the costs of an experiment. I had to train myself to remember to include these insights as part of both the evaluation and the review of the investment.

So, there you have it, a simple yet effective way to budget for experimentation. All you have to do is bring your finance team and senior leadership along on the journey with you. Allow for a 90/10 rule in budgeting (or 95/5 if you have an overly nervous CFO), then remember to include the insights gained when explaining the value of running the experiment.

What next? Well, now we get to the exciting part of the book, the practical examples of experiments that you can either try, or use an inspiration for your own experiments.

But before we do, we need to have a quick look back at some of the things we covered in section two.

SECTION TWO SUMMARY

Well, my experimentation ninjas, you have made it to the last section of the book and now you not only have a solid framework for experimentation (which you can choose to use or modify to suit your own needs), but you also have a good understanding of the mindset required to successfully implement it. Hopefully, you will also have with some choice ways to help cultivate that mindset. At this point, let's have a quick look at some of the key takeouts from section two, 'The Experimental Mindset.'

Find your cues – One of the important traits you need for experimentation is fortitude (or the ability to hold strong in adverse conditions). One of the ways to cultivate this is to train your brain to respond to cues. Spend some time working out your own cues. Start documenting what you are wearing, feeling, saying, and surrounded by when you are feeling particularly strong. This will help you to understand what your brain is associating with strength and it will give you some good insight into how to program your own mind.

Create a keystone habit – Curiosity is not only an important factor in experimentation, but an important aspect in being a decent person. Did you know that children tend to ask up to 73 questions a day? Channel your inner four-year-old and constantly ask yourself (and others) "why, why, and why." Strengthning your own curiosity will be a powerful habit to create.

Own imposter syndrome – Remember how we talked about the fact that most of us doubt our own abilities? Well, a key point in that fact is the word 'most.' It is time for us to embrace imposter syndrome and realise that the people we tend to look up to are just as insecure as we are. Own your own confidence.

Know your biases – We all have biases... that is just a fact of being human. Make it part of your daily or weekly routine to investigate the various types of cognitive bias. Remember, knowledge is power!

Ask yourself the hard questions – Understanding cognitive

bias is only the first step in debiasing our brains. One of the most important things we can do is ask ourselves the hard questions. Are we subconsciously affecting the results of an experiment? Are we chasing the wins instead of the insights? Keep yourself honest with a regular dose of reality checking.

Time to rebudget – Experimentation is a key to finding new markets, opportunities, and ways to win. Start to look at your digital marketing budgets with a view to introducing the 90/10 rule (or 95/5 if you have a nervous CFO). Look at how you can allocate 10% of your budget for each line item so that you can conduct experiments in each channel. It will pay dividends very quickly.

Now it is time for the section you have all waited so patiently for: the experiments!

THE

EXPERIMENTS

"With experimentation comes surprise and discovery."
Kim Lee Kho

THE EXPERIMENTS

Okay, now it is time for you to don your white lab coats, fire up the Bunsen burner, and get ready to have some fun.

This is the part of the book where you get some practical experiments that you can try. The goal here is to inspire you to think differently. Some of these experiments will not suit your business needs or any challenges you have in your organisation or industry. They will, however, have elements that can inspire you to find experiments that will work for you. To help you out, I have given five experiments that I have personally conducted. These range from very simple to slightly more obscure. Again, they are designed to get you to think differently.

Additionally, I have a real treat. I have interviewed some

of the best digital marketing talent in the world and included some wise words on experimentation, as well as five experiments from each of them. We have Michael Brenner form West Chester, Pennsylvania in the United States of America, Ciaran Rogers from Portsmouth in the United Kingdom, and Tim Pointer from my hometown of Wellington, New Zealand.

Enjoy, and let me know on social how you get on with the experiments or any experiments you come up with yourself.

So, let's have a look at my pick of the experiments.

Experiment 1 - Minimum Effort

Challenge: Click-through rates on our Call To Action are not as high as we would like. Consumer feedback indicates that there is some hesitation to click on our "Get a quote" or "Sign up here" buttons.

Hypothesis: Our hypothesis is that the hesitation could be due to a perception that it may be complicated, mentally taxing, or that it may take too long. If we reduce cerebral bandwidth by quantifying the effort required directly in the Call To Action, we would see an increase in conversion.

Details: This is a relatively simple one to test. The goal is to add the effort required to the Call To Action itself. As an example, if our CTA was "Get a quote," we could A/B test "Get an instant quote." If the Call To Action was to "Sign up here," we could add another line to say, "It takes less than a minute."

The idea, of course, is to reduce the amount of doubt about what happens when you click on a CTA. The more you feel you know (like the effort required), the more at ease consumers will be about clicking the button.

You can run this as an A/B test or, if you are not set up with an A/B testing tool, then run it as a block test. To do that, keep a tight record on the conversion rates by channel with the current CTA, then change to the new one and run the experiment over a closed period of time and compare the conversion rates back to the control.

Pay close attention to what channel the traffic and conversions come from to ensure you do not skew the experiment with any campaigns you have in market that may have a higher or lower intent than your control.

Experiment 2 - Latest and Greatest

Challenge: We want to get different offers out to consumers that are early adopters.

Hypothesis: If we go out to early adopters of technology with more personalised messaging, we will get higher than average engagement.

Details: This is an interesting experiment that may not suit most of you. The goal is to get targeted ads in front of early technology adopters. To run this experiment, look at whatever the latest "hot" mobile device version is coming into market. You can run targeted Facebook ads based on users that have accessed Facebook on specific device models.

There are two things to consider here. One is the messaging. If you truly are getting in front of early adopters, then trial messages that allude to "exclusivity" or "being the first."

The second consideration is that the device they access from may not be an accurate measure of early adoption. You need to look at very tight timeframes just as the mobile device is launched, and it has to be a model that is not necessarily just the latest version. Where this works well is when a brand like Apple comes out with the latest version of their device and at the same time releases a more expensive elite model. A good example of this was when the major mobile brands started launching 'Plus' versions of their devices.

Run your ads directly to that small group of users and compare the conversion rates with your control (standard ad conversion rates).

Experiment 3 - Just the Text

Challenge: Open rates on email campaigns are not as high as we would like.

Hypothesis: Templated HTML emails are becoming white noise amongst the hundreds of solicitation emails consumers regularly receive. If we change tactics and do away with HTML emails and go instead to a more personalised text-based email, we should cut through the noise.

Details: This is an easy one to test. Simply design a version of your email template that is only text-based. Ensure that visually it more closely resembles a standard email that someone would receive from a friend and A/B test against your current template.

Experiment 4 - Proof I'm Social

Challenge: We want to drive a higher conversion rate from our purchase page on our website.

Hypothesis: We have a hypothesis that there are too many different options on the purchase page for our products. This could be resulting in 'Choice Blindness.' If we help our website visitors to eliminate most of the choices by providing social proof, we should see more decisive behaviours and, as a result, a higher conversion rate.

Details: This is an experiment that will require some background work. You will need to have a good understanding of what options your customers usually choose and why. Once you know, the goal will be to test a product page that highlights which option 'People Like You' usually choose (where the people like you is the customer, not the experimenter... just thought I should clarify).

Once you have set up the new product page, do an A/B test in one of your digital channels. Paid search is usually a good one to try this with, as the visitors from paid search are usually higher in intent because they are actively looking for a solution. Run two different ads, both going to the separate landing pages. Once you have enough data from the experiment, you will want to check the conversion rate results as well as what ratio of the visitors chose the 'people like you' option.

Experiment 5 - Pronouns

Challenge: We want to increase the amount of people who make use of our lead magnet (this could be getting an online quote or signing up for an account).

Hypothesis: Changing the pronoun used for our lead magnets could affect the propensity for a user to take action.

Details: This is a very simple test that you will want to run multiple A/B tests against your current Call To Action wording for your lead magnet.

You simply change the pronoun used in the wording for the CTA. For example, if you have "Get a quote" you could change this to "Get your quote" or "Get my quote." Similarly, if you want them to sign up for an account, you could change "Create an account" to either "Create your account" or "Create my account."

Test each of the wording changes against your current wording to test conversion rates. You may be surprised at the results.

Bonus Experiment - PR Candy

Challenge: We need to increase our external Public Relations coverage.

Hypothesis: We can increase the perception of us as thought leaders by surveying consumers (or other businesses if you are a B2B business) and using that content to generate PR.

Details: This is a bonus experiment that can produce multiple benefits. To execute is easy... you just need to survey as many of your target market as possible. I won't get into the specifics of how you survey them, as the best way to do this will depend on your target market.

The difficult part of this experiment is in crafting the questions. Ideally, you want to have between five to seven questions. Each question should be designed with multiple purposes in mind. Each question should form a piece of commentary on the industry. What I mean by this is that each question should be able to form an insight into the state of your industry. This will mean that each question will allow you to have a press release just from the results of that one question.

Additionally, each question should be designed to understand more about the purchase decisions or behaviours of your target market. The reason for this is so that you can retarget each of the users that answer questions in various ways to talk directly to their issues or concerns. This will mean that not only do you generate PR from the exercise, but you could also potentially generate some sales.

The other thing to consider with the questions is what you do with them next. Think about the press releases, infographics, and social content that you can generate from each question. Just remember, it is easy to position yourself as a thought leader when you are talking about hard facts (or in this case, data-backed insights).

CIARAN ROGERS

For any digital marketer familiar with podcasts, you will no doubt be acquainted with Ciaran Rogers. In addition to being a best-selling author of the Complete Guide to Search Engine Optimisation, Ciaran also produces and co-hosts The Digital Marketing Podcast, Target Internet's top 10 iTunes podcast (and one of my personal favourites).

Born and based in the United Kingdom, Ciaran has over 21 years of experience in Digital Marketing and is the Marketing Director at Target Internet, a digital training agency offering straightforward and easy to understand digital marketing advice.

Something that became very obvious when interviewing Ciaran for this book was his passion for both Digital Marketing and experimentation. Our interview went on for quite some time, as we both went down a rabbit hole of different examples and analogies (along with a large dose of laughter from the two of us).

Ciaran has helped organisations of all types to use digital marketing effectively, working with a wide range of businesses, from start-ups through to global clients. His career has covered work in both B2B and B2C markets, as well as work for nonprofit organisations. He has worked for and trained a large number of international brands including QA, Liz Earle, Elemis, Time to Spa, UKSA, Jubilee Sailing Trust, The Sustainable Food Trust, Hershesons Bliss, REN Skincare, and FatFace.

One thing that really stands out with Ciaran is his practical and hands-on approach. He brings best practice techniques from his many years working for a broad range of international clients across the full range of digital marketing techniques. With such a wealth of practical digital marketing experience, he is skilled in both the technical and business aspects of digital marketing, meaning he can bridge the gap between the two and make the best use of the tools and technology available.

Follow Ciaran on Twitter (@Ciaraniow) and LinkedIn https://www.linkedin.com/in/ciaranrogers/

Ciaran Rogers on experimentation:

So I think, for me, experimentation is about trying to improve on what I've done before. It's a way of pitching myself against myself. A lot of people, when they first start to experiment, try to beat the competition. For me, I realized that chasing the competition wasn't radical enough. I mean, it didn't really take me to a new, exciting place. Everybody ends up beating themselves over the head with the same stick. To compete against yourself though, that is about continual improvement, and it is about comparing an experiment with your previous experiments. If you compare this month this year, with the same month last year, you can see how much you've improved. I use that as a benchmark.

Experimentation is also a great opportunity to understand your customer base a lot more than you think you know. It enables you to understand how they want to be helped and how you can help them. To do that though, you need to see how they think and how they behave. You can only really do that through experiments. Understanding this is so important; there have been so many times that I have had my ass whipped by the customers because I arrogantly went out with an experiment I thought was going to show a certain result. In a lot of cases, the more certain I am, the more wrong I am. So, you learn, and it's a continual learning process.

It's about finding better ways of doing things, finding more efficient ways of operating. I think marketing could be seen as getting others (customers) to do what your company wants them to do. We all fall into that trap at times. In fact, many CEO's I've worked with seem to think like that, unless they are in a marketing function. But the truth is, it doesn't actually work like that. As a marketer, you have to find ways to bridge that all-important gap between what the company wants to bang on about and what the market wants to actually listen to and engage with.

I love case studies like Nike. Think to yourself, what do they do? They make sports gear, right?

But that's not how they see their mission. They've got a branding strategy statement, which goes along the lines of "we want to help our customers reach their true athletic potential." That's why they get involved in all these amazing things like fitness trackers and apps to help you do that. It's totally about what the customer wants. Because, actually, if I'm buying Nike kit, it's because I want to realize my true athletic potential, whether I am an armchair athlete or a pro.

One of the best pieces of advice I can give to digital marketers doing experimentation is about knowing what to experiment with. Just because something didn't work before, that doesn't mean you can close the book on it. It might be that you've only slightly missed the mark.

Let me give you an analogy. I remember there was this great time management course I did years ago by a chap called Mark Joyner. Its full name wass "Simpleology, the simple science of getting what you want." You may very well laugh at that, but young Ciaran fell for it hook line and sinker. This was the very early days of podcasting, long before iTunes and iPods. I had to download the audio onto a CD and play it in my car. Anyway, one of the things Mark taught in his course was to "See your target clearly and hit it until you hit it." That was one of the most important lessons for me. When you have a constantly moving target, that becomes increasingly difficult, right?

What we experiment with now, we're actually dealing with a different mindset and a different group of customers from what we experimented with a few months ago. That ups the ante, right?

Think about how an archer hits his target. If the archer just goes slightly left at the bullseye, then he knows he was close. Now, in marketing experimentation, you don't know. If you don't hit it and kill it, it looks like it failed. In reality, you could be really close to the bullseye. Just a few small adjustments would make a difference, right? As marketers, we constantly throw the baby out with the bathwater. That's why I think if you're really studying your market, and really studying your customer, you do get a bit of an innate sense of how close to the mark you were, and whether to just walk away and start again, or keep going and try a few variations around it. But it takes time and practice to know what to experiment with. I think it's good to pick radically difficult things to test if you can, but there does need to be a sense of logic behind that. You can't just do it to be radical or you're gonna get spanked.

Here are some examples of experiments I recommend:

Experiment 1 - Leaky Bucket

Challenge: All of us have some form of funnel to drive users through our website. For some reason, we're all happy to pour a lot more water (leads) into that funnel so that we can get more out of the bottom, right? But the reality is that most funnels are full of leaks. So rather than pour more water in the funnel to get more out, we want to plug the holes.

Hypothesis: Understanding the user journey and experience personally will help to find holes in our leaky funnel.

Details: This experiment is about understanding the experience for users moving through your online funnel. You can perform this easily with just a PC, tablet, and mobile phone. However, I like to do this with some form of screen recording software. The idea is simple: you systematically go through the user journey and look at all of your key conversion points. This will include all landing pages, lead forms, and calls to action. The goal here is to walk in your customer's shoes to see what the experience is like. You will be surprised at what you find and what obstacles we accidentally put in the way of our users.

I would do this on a range of devices and types. Laptop, desktop, Mac, iOS devices, Android devices, and on a reasonable-sized tablet as well. Have a look at the experience on each of the devices and note what you find. I've never done this and not found something that like is gobsmackingly really brilliant.

Experiment 2 - Ugly Baby

Challenge: No one wants to admit that their baby's ugly. Right? The reality is, no website is perfect and, as with the 'Leaky Bucket' experiment, we could all do better at fixing the holes.

Hypothesis: Getting usability feedback from users will identify actionable areas to improve our website.

Details: This experiment is relatively easy to run but requires a small amount of investment. The goal is simple: to have users go through a predefined user journey and to record the experience and their feedback.

For this type of experiment, I've previously used a service called WhatUsersDo; however, there are many others such as UserSnap and Usability Testing Exchange. These services have an army of a testers from lots of different demographic profiles that can test your website and funnel. They'll get you to set up an experiment with them, will ask a few qualifying questions, and, depending on the answers to that, will match you with the right audience.

You ideally want to recruit a set of maybe three to five testers. You set them a task such as "find and purchase x on my website." The users will then go to your website, navigate through, and, as they do this, they will talk you through what they're thinking. So you get back a recording, not just of what they did, but also of their thoughts. This is the key: there's lots of website recording software that will measure what people do and some you could see their mouse moving on the screen. But here you get to hear their thoughts as well, and it's brilliant.

So you'll get back three to five recordings for each experiment. It can go through and you can annotate and timestamp and highlight key moments. And it's an element of sometimes they will just be putting their own perspective on it, but more often than not, you'll see commonality. See, when you get two or three of them mentioned the same thing. It's like, "Yeah, Houston, we've got problem here" and it is tremendously powerful.

Experiment 3 - Radical PPC

Challenge: How do we compete for Pay Per Click advertising in an already crowded space? We all know that we should review all the important keyword landscapes. Look at what our competitors are doing, what are their key calls to action? We all create our own variations on those CTAs. I think in a lot of keyword spaces, everybody's just really locked in to doing the same thing. So how do we stand out?

Hypothesis: If we create a radically different Pay Per Click ad, we can stand out from the white noise.

Details: Sometimes doing this can be a real breakthrough; it can be really big.

The execution of this is relatively simple. You first want a clear picture of what your competitors are doing, what their creative is, what their call to action and USP are. Now, test an ad that is radically different to anything you have done before. Test this as a separate ad unit and see what results you get.

Look, it doesn't always work, but if you're setting it against the run of the mill stuff that you would have run anyway, what's the harm?

Experiment 4 - Let's Get Meta

Challenge: We want to increase engagement through our organic search results. This in turn will increase our relevancy scores in Google and result in better organic search ranking. Click-through rates are one of the key principles of Google's algorithm.

Hypothesis: If we improve your web page titles and meta descriptions and write them from a customer's perspective, we will see increased engagement. If we can get across the promise of what's available behind a click, more people will click it.

Details: For years I've been reading what all the experts were saying: "Yeah, your meta descriptions, they're not used as part of the Google algorithm" and "You don't keyword spam in your meta descriptions because it's pointless and it looks bad." I agree with both of these comments. But then I realised, although Google doesn't analyze the text of your meta description, customers read it and Google analyzes what the customers do. Titles in your meta descriptions are effectively free ads.

The principle of this experiment is simple: just change the meta titles and descriptions for your key sales pages to help describe what is behind that click. Describe what they will get. Too often we use specific brand words or descriptions hoping to get ranked for those terms. However, if we focus on what the customer needs, we will get far better results.

You will be surprised how good the results can be from this type of experiment.

Experiment 5 - No More Emails

Challenge: We have no true idea what effect email blasts have on other channels.

Hypothesis: Email has an attribution effect on other digital channels, and by pausing activity in that channel we will have a negative result on the other digital activity, but it will also help us to understand the true attribution rate.

Details: This is a complex experiment and not for the faint of heart. I am using emails here as an example; however, you could substitute most digital activity to measure the attribution effect. The goal of this experiment sounds simple. You want to pause activity in a digital channel (in this case it is email traffic, as it is easiest to pause) and to look at the flow-on effect through all of your other channels.

This is a complex one to measure, but it can produce interesting results. Before you begin, you want to understand month on month traffic trends per channel. You want to understand any seasonal changes that may arise while you are mid-experiment, and you will need to be very aware of any market trends or external activity that could affect the results.

Then you need to summon the courage to push pause on your email activity for a set period of time. Measure what happens to both the traffic per channel and the conversion rates in each channel. This will help to give you a base understanding of how much effect your email activity has on other channels.

This experiment can be particularly important if you have a lot of digital activity in market and want to understand what you can change with minimal impact.

MICHAEL BRENNER

Michael Brenner is a globally recognized keynote speaker on leadership, culture, and marketing. Michael co-authored the bestselling books *The Content Formula* and *Digital Marketing Growth Hacks* and has written more than 1,000 articles for *The Economist, The Guardian, Forbes, Entrepreneur Magazine* and more.

If you have ever had the pleasure to hear him speak, you will understand why, for the past two years running, Michael has been named a Top Business Speaker by *The Huffington Post* as well as a top CMO Influencer by *Forbes*.

Over the last two decades, Michael has championed a customer-centric approach at organizations large and small. He led sales and marketing for software companies like Nielsen and FullTilt. As an executive at ICR, SAP, and Newscred, Michael's innovative leadership resulted in massive growth. His workshops and keynotes for Fortune 500 brands and tiny startups have inspired profound personal and professional change.

Michael is someone that I have the immense honor and pleasure to be able to call a mentor of mine. It seems that everytime I connect with Michael, I come away both inspired and with an eerie sense of confidence and calm.

Today, Michael lives in West Chester, PA with his wife and four children. He is the CEO of Marketing Insider Group, where he helps brands to create content that converts and delivers presentations that connect at events all over the world. Michael shares his passion on leadership and marketing strategies to help people like you deliver better customer value and improved business impact.

Follow Michael on Twitter (@BrennerMichael) and LinkedIn https://www.linkedin.com/in/michaelbrenner/

Michael Brenner on experimentation:

To me, experimentation is an opportunity to learn what you are good at doing or have the most fun doing and to learn what the world wants from you, and those elements of whatever you are doing that produce the best results. One of the biggest reasons that marketing either struggles to work in an organisation or proves its value is that too many marketers (particularly senior marketers) walk into a situation thinking we either know or can think through (or brainstorm) the big idea that is going to solve all of the problems.

I actually look at marketing as one big experiment every single day. Every day is a chance to test a new marketing concept. A good example of this is the articles that I publish on my website. I try to publish one or two articles every single day from Monday to Thursday. For me, I look at every article to see if it is going to be better than the article yesterday. I look to see if it is going to be better than the one I wrote weeks ago… am I going to get a new winner? So, for me, marketing is experimentation. Every day is another opportunity to gain a new insight.

Experimentation also gives us a competitive advantage. It allows us to gain the knowledge needed to produce the best results for the least amount of resources (time, money, anxiety) invested.

Experimentation is not always easy though. In fact, the biggest challenge is often in showing others why you need to have an experimentation mindset in the first place. As a consultant in content marketing and digital marketing strategy, I'm often surprised by the number of senior marketers who think they know best. So many leaders think that it is the thought inside their head that leads to success. The challenge with experimentation is convincing others, especially powerful stakeholders, that we do experimentation because we don't know everything, we don't know what our audience wants, and that the world is constantly changing.

The biggest advice I can give to marketers is that everything is an experiment. I'm a big believer that the idea of "campaigns" is truly dead. I believe in always-on marketing. The definition of a campaign almost implies it is for a specific period of time. Campaigns mean you have to guess which audience will want which piece of content or creative, on which channel, and hope that it works. With always-on approaches, every hour of every day is an opportunity to experiment. Publish something every day. Test something every week.

In my first leadership role in digital marketing, I was responsible for a multi-million-dollar budget for SAP North America. We tested everything. And we used to make simple bets about which content, channel, publisher, etc. would produce the best results. The funniest thing is that we were almost always wrong. The saddest thing is that we kept getting asked (by sales and product teams) to push content into channels we knew wouldn't work. But, hey, in the world of always-on experiments, you have to allow everything to come into the tests. The beauty of experimentation is that we don't have to say "no" to them. We can run a series of experiments and use the results and the insights to prove or disprove the value of each of those channels.

Here are some examples of experiments I recommend:

Experiment 1 - Headline Act

Challenge: We want more people to view our content. Research shows that 80% of people that land on your site click through to a web page or see your email, and they will only read the headline and then bounce.

Hypothesis: Different headlines will produce stronger results and more cut-through for our content marketing efforts.

Details: Spend the time testing headlines for your content. I have found that it often takes three to five rapid fire split test experiments on headlines before you get the best results.

A good way to run this is during an email blast. Take 10% of your audience and split them 50/50. Test two different headlines for an article with each half of the 10%.

Then take another 10% of your base and split test the winner of the first experiment with a new headline. If you repeat this five times, you have experimented on 50% of your list. You can then go out to the remaining 50% with the strongest headline possible.

This experiment can see up to a hundred times improvement in click-through rate and engagement rate.

Experiment 2 - Picture This

Challenge: We want increased engagement with our content marketing efforts. Research shows that marketing content that has imagery is likely to have twice the engagement rate to content that does not. We are becoming a more visually engaged society, so these figures will increase even more over time.

Hypothesis: Different images in our content will produce stronger results and more cut-through for our content marketing efforts.

Details: Spend the time testing different images for your content. As with the Headline Act experiment, it often takes three to five rapid fire split test experiments on images before you get the best results.

A good way to run this is doing traffic-based split tests to a blog. Over the period of a day, run a 50/50 split test between two different images for the same article. See which test has the most amount of people clicking on that article and which has the highest engagement rate.

An interesting point you may find with this experiment is that images with faces on may perform better. Likewise, images where people are looking directly at you, or images with kids in them may also perform particularly well.

Another thing you could try here is for articles that are about particular concepts such as digital transformation. Try showing images that are far afield from the topic or concept. As an example, for the article on digital transformation, you could show an image of a painting that is getting rained on and changing. Those images can sometimes perform better than a traditional digital transformation image such as a robot.

Experiment 3 - Color Me Impressed

Challenge: We want to increase the cut-through of our marketing elements.

Hypothesis: Color has surprising impact on everything. I have seen massive changes in measurable components based on the simple changing of color. Our hypothesis is that by using secondary or tertiary colors from our color palette, we can increase engagement with marketing elements.

Details: Run an experiment using your secondary or tertiary colors on elements of your digital marketing. The obvious starting point here is with elements such as email banners and Call To Action (CTA) buttons.

You can easily test this using a A/B options. For email banners, you can simply split test the different color options to a percentage of you user base, seeing which color performs best. For CTA buttons, you can use A/B testing solutions such as VWO, Optimizely, or Omniconvert. Simply set an alternate version of the CTA button using the secondary or tertiary colour options, then split test to see which performs best.

You can also test other marketing elements such as banner ads, social content, ebook covers, and more. Everything is an opportunity to test the impact of color.

One thing to note is to try and stay on brand as much as possible. There is a lot of science behind the psychology of color, but just because the Pantone color of the year was a purple last year, it doesn't mean I am going to change all of my banner imagery to purple.

Experiment 4 - Pole Position

Challenge: We spend a lot of time and effort on our website and landing pages and want to ensure we are optimising for the best results in reach, engagement, and conversion.

Hypothesis: I believe we make instant decisions about a brand the second we land on their website. So the colors, fonts, and the images we use are all important. But one of the biggest opportunities for testing is the layout of your pages. Optimising the layout of a page can dramatically increase the reach, the engagement, and the conversion rates of visitors to the site.

Details: Many folks I know just take the standard template they get from their CMS or their marketing automation provider. But you can experiment on where things go on the page. I used to use Omniture, which is now part of Adobe Marketing Cloud. Omniture used the concept of recipes and ingredients, and basically you can turn every section of a website into a component to be tested.

For this experiment, I like to test the position of a number of elements such as hero images, CTAs, copy blocks, lead magnets, banner ads, top bars, pop-ups, even navigation elements.

The best way to test these is as traditional Conversion Rate Optimisation (CRO) tests. Similar to the 'Color Me Impressed' experiment, you can use the A/B testing tools to see what difference it makes to conversion rates when you move elements around the page.

For this type of experiment, you may want to go beyond just conversion rate as a measure of success though. There is a danger that experimenting purely on conversion rate will mean that promotional elements will be too front and centre. We used a concept called Blended Metric, which used a 30-40-30 mix of reach, engagement, and conversion to find the right balance and the right mix for the page.

Experiment 5 - Filtered View

Challenge: We live in a world where your audience is trying to avoid marketers as much as possible and hide their personal information in as many ways as they can. This behaviour is resulting in demographic-based lists and filters not performing as well as they used to.

Hypothesis: If we can filter our audience based on intent and/or interest, we can get a better response than demographic-based filtering.

Details: So for this experiment, you want to test intent-based or interest-based filters. To do this, you may want to work with third-party-based data management services such as BlueKai. By using a combination of pixeling your website and using these third-party services, you can build audiences for your content around context and intent. These services look at their engagement patterns and interests to enable you to be matched with an audience that is most relevant to your content or offering.

You can then use these lists to test different content on topics and themes through Facebook marketing.

There are a few caveats with this experiment. First of all, this is an experiment that will require some effort and investment up front if you want to use services such as BlueKai.

Secondly, you need to think seriously about the privacy implications with this. Be very upfront and clear in your terms and conditions about what you are using the data for.

TIM POINTER

Tim is the award-winning co-founder and CEO of Uprise Digital, a bottom-line marketing company here in Wellington, New Zealand that links their business model directly to the success of their clients.

With over a decade's experience in digital marketing, Tim started Uprise Digital 10 years ago with his co-founder Matt Rowe. They took the company from a two-man band in his parents' spare bedroom, to a team of 32 and one of New Zealand's largest and most well-regarded digital performance agencies, with clients around the world. In addition to a trophy cabinet full of awards, Uprise has been recognised as a Deloitte Fast 500 Asia Pacific company in 2014, 2015, and 2016.

The word 'Disruptor' gets thrown around far too quickly. However, in Tim's case, this is pretty much the only way to describe his impact on the marketing landscape in New Zealand.

Tim has been honored in the *Forbes* 30 Under 30 list for Asia Pacific in 2016. In fact, Tim was the only New Zealander to be recognised in the prestigious list as a young innovator and leader in media, marketing, and advertising in Asia. The criteria for honorees included leadership and disruption in their field; entrepreneurial mind-set and results; and the likelihood of changing the field in the next half-century, something that is apparent when you meet Tim.

If you have ever had the pleasure of talking digital marketing with Tim over a pint or three, you will know two things: one, he has a passion to challenge the norms of the industry (or as Tim puts it "un-f#@king the marketing industry") and two, that passion is so contagious that you may just get asked to keep the noise down by a nearby hens party (I can neither confirm nor deny if this has ever happened to us).

Follow Tim on Twitter (@PointerTim) and LinkedIn https://www.linkedin.com/in/timpointer/

Tim Pointer on experimentation:

The internet as we know it today, is almost entirely supported by paid advertising or some form of commerce. The profits are reinvested into innovation and building a better experience. You can see this in how Google makes 89% of its revenue from ads and Facebook makes 93% of its revenue from advertising. So when you have that kind of fierce competition in market, fighting over the same advertising dollar, you will find it breeds innovation. Of course it's no surprise to see these media companies (yes we're talking about Google and Facebook) are investing so aggressively in this space. This investment is creating new advertising opportunities weekly, if not daily, to reach your customers more effectively. For that very reason, experimentation should be a 'must have' if you want to win, but also at some level, if you want to survive.

The ways of connecting with customers are becoming more advanced than ever, and if organisations aren't trying and testing new things, it is leaving them (particularly bigger organisations) exposed. Any new business can come in with a more targeted approach, better value proposition and engage with their customers better. We are seeing this time and time again with new players (often well funded) coming into markets that, digitally speaking, are behind the times and are creating billion-dollar businesses in a couple of years. There is basically so much innovation that you have to test or experiment just to stay ahead of your competitors, because if you don't they, or someone, will.

I am also astounded at how the digital channel has revolutionised market testing. It is probably the only advertising channel that has been created that allows us to rapidly test ideas, concepts, and research in a scalable, low cost way. This is something that a lot of people miss and as a result is highly underutilised. Experimentation (particularly in digital) is an engine for getting great insights on your customers.

One of the common mistakes in experimentation is that a lot of people focus purely on metrics. You will hear them say, "I am doing this to get more [insert something they think is important]... leads, customers, revenue." That is definitely one of the advantages of experimentation, but the mistake comes when they are focused only on the short term. Instead they need to focus on what they are learning about their customers, not just the metrics themselves. These customer insights should be able to be amplified in other areas of the business (marketing, sales, customer service) to create exponential value. When you add up all of these insights, this is when you end up with an exponential shift.

The best thing that you can do with experimentation is to just start. The more testing you do, literally, the better you get at it. When you run experiments, you are just being exposed to so much insight about your customers and it is really difficult to get that much experience any other way. Many people read blogs or case studies to try and get the same understanding or insight, not knowing that the end result of that case study may have involved multiple tests and refinements to lead to that insight. You cannot underestimate how powerful the learnings from each of those tests could be. So just start, because you will quickly accumulate a wealth of knowledge.

Here are some examples of experiments I recommend:

Experiment 1 - Vary Painful

Challenge: Clients often have products and services that, although may be the same solution, will have very different value propositions either to the same customer audience or to different audiences.

Hypothesis: We believe that testing two different value proposition variants for the largest digital audience will result in an increase in click-through rate and conversions.

Details: For this experiment, test AdWords ad copy with two different variants on the largest volume non-brand keyword groups. Those variants should be completely different value propositions talking to different pain points.

Keep track of the click-through rate and conversion rate for four weeks (time depending on click volume).

Experiment 2 - Get Pointy

Challenge: Customers who are in the consideration or buying phase need to see the benefit of a product or service before they convert. The benefits of a product or service need to be clear and easily findable on a website or landing page.

Hypothesis: We believe that punchy, benefits-based messaging for customers who are in the consideration and buying phases will result in a higher conversion rate.

Details: For this experiment, test landing page copy with three to four clear bullet points positioned before the call to action.

Keep track of the conversion rate and heat mapping for four weeks (time depending on click volume).

Experiment 3 - Facebook is Weird

Challenge: Of all the paid channels, traffic that comes in from Google often has the highest engagement due to the nature of channels being pull marketing (i.e., customers looking for you).

Paid Facebook traffic can be 40% less engaged (and converting) than paid Google traffic.

Hypothesis: We believe that a specific landing page for Facebook traffic with a different call to action specifically for the Facebook paid traffic will result in a higher-engaging page (conversion rate).

Details: For this experiment, create a custom landing page specifically for traffic from Facebook. On the landing page design, ensure it has a low scroll profile and a call to action to download an information resource.

Keep track of the conversion rate and heat mapping for four weeks (time depending on click volume).

Experiment 4 - No Commitment

Challenge: The wording around the call to action is incredibly important. Non-committal wording can increase conversion rates in markets where they are making a high-consideration purchase.

Hypothesis: We believe that testing two different ad copy and landing page variants for AdWords traffic and the key CTA landing pages will result in a higher click-through rate and conversion rate.

Details: For this experiment, test ad copy variants using non-committal wording. As an example, you can change 'Get a quote' to 'Compare a quote' on all visitors in AdWords and put the CTA button on the landing page.

Keep track of the click-through rate and conversion rate for four weeks (time depending on click volume).

Experiment 5 - Simple Signup

Challenge: The longer the form, the lower the conversion rates. Visitors are less inclined to give out personal information unless they are ready to buy. Of all the personal information, an email address is what people are willing to give up the easiest

Hypothesis: We believe a smaller sign-up form for visitors not ready to buy will result in a higher conversion rate.

Details: For this experiment, we want to create a simple sign-up form that only asks for an email address. Test this form on visitors (or segments) who are disproportionately underperforming.

Keep track of the conversion rate for four weeks (time depending on click volume).

FIN

There you have it folks, you have made it all the way through my first ever book. Now you should have a good understanding of a framework you can use for bringing experimentation to digital marketing, what mindset you require to successfully implement it, and some practical experiments to try.

Now it is your turn. Hit me up on social media to ask me any questions and to let me know how your experimentation adventure plays out.

Oh, and thank you for taking the time to read my book. I hope you got as much out of it as the fun I had writing it.

Vince

ABOUT THE AUTHOR

An award-winning marketer and a sought-after public speaker, Vince Warnock has been inducted into the 2018 Fearless50, a program to recognize the top 50 marketers in the world who are driving bold, fearless marketing and digital transformation.

Vince has an eclectic background, training as an Electronics and Computer Engineer before broadening into sound engineering, radio announcing, web development, and film until, eventually, marketing.

Currently Chief Marketing Officer at Cigna Life Insurance and previously the co-founder of high growth tech startup Common Ledger, with his wealth of knowledge and experience in the marketing industry, Vince gives back regularly through his work with the Marketing Association and as a mentor and tutor.

Feel free to reach out to Vince on social media at:

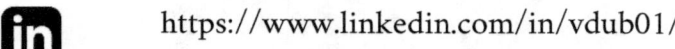 https://www.linkedin.com/in/vdub01/

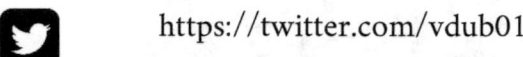 https://twitter.com/vdub01

And don't forget to sign up to the newsletter if you want more inspiration and experiments to try at:

www.chasingtheinsights.com

Thanks for reading! Please add a short review on Amazon and let me know what you thought!

Thanks, and good luck!
Vince Warnock